How to Erase Bad Credit

written by **Stanley R. Stern**, Esq. & **David Waldman**, Esq.

Are you one of the thousands upon thousands of Americans who are rejected for credit?

Are you frustrated and feel that you have nowhere to turn for advice and guidance?

NOW!!! You can save hundreds of dollars or more on attorney's fees and credit repair clinics with this kit.

DO YOU WANT TO FIGHT BACK?

Challenge the credit giants that control your financial future with this one of a kind manual.

Easy to use legal forms are enclosed with step by step instructions to repair your credit status.

A credit application is included for you to apply for a VISA or Mastercard.

VALID IN ALL 50 STATES

Copyright 1990 by D. Waldman

How To Erase Bad Credit

Bad Credit Histories Can Be Erased Or Rewritten! 2

You Can Help Yourself 2

This Manual Is Better Than So-Called Credit Repair Clinics 2

List Of Forms 4

Beware Of Credit Fraud 5

Beware Of Innocent Errors 6

An Overview Of The Organizational Structure Of This Manual 7

What Is Credit? 8

The Importance Of Your Credit File 8

What Information Is Stored In Your Credit File 8

Part II - The Credit System Framework 10

The Need For Credit Information 10

Credit Reporting Agencies 10

Part III - Overview Of The Fair Credit Reporting Act 11

Where Do Credit Reporting Agencies Get Their Information? 11

How Accurate Is Your Credit File? 11

The Consumer Report 11

What To Do When You Receive Notice Of Rejection Of Credit 11

A Note On Perseverance 12

How To Add New Data To Your Consumer Report 12

How Long Can Negative Adverse Information Remain
On Your Consumer Report? 12

How To Erase Bad Credit

How To Remove Accurate But Negative Information From
Your Credit Report 13

How To Find Your Credit Reporting Agency 13

Directory Of Credit Bureau Offices 14

How To Obtain A Copy Of Your Consumer Report 16

A Sample TRW Credit Report 17

How To Read Your TRW Credit Report 18

Part IV - How To Deal With Creditors 21

How To Deal With Judgment Creditors 21

How To Handle Tax Liens 22

State & Local Tax Liens 22

Federal Taxes 23

It Is Possible To Compromise Your Tax Liability With The IRS 23

Instructions For Offer In Compromise - Form 656 23

How To Deal With Lawsuits 25

How To Re-Open Default Judgments 25

Priority Of Payment To Creditors 26

How To Deal With Credit Reporting Agencies 26

Part V - Detailed Discussion Of The Finer Points Of The Fair
Credit Reporting Act 27

Consumer Credit Protection - Subchapter III Credit Reporting Agencies 28

Findings Of Congress 36

Congress' Purposes 36

How To Erase Bad Credit

Importance Of Congress' Findings And Statement Of Purpose 36

You Are A Consumer! 36

Who Can Get A Copy Of Your Consumer Credit Report 36

Examples Of What Are And Are Not Consumer Reports 37

Who Is A Consumer Reporting Agency? 37

Compliance Procedures Of Credit Reporting Agencies 37

Agency's Duty To Update Obsolete Information 38

What Constitutes Obsolete Information 38

Obsolete & Adverse Information Chart 39

Disclosures To You Of Your Files By A Consumer Reporting Agency 40

Notification To Consumer Of Adverse Action By User Of A
Consumer Report 40

Conditions And Charges A Consumer Reporting Agency May
Set Prior To Its Duty To Disclosure To You Of Your File 40

Charges 41

Credit Reporting Agency Fee Chart 42

Procedure In The Case Of Disputed Accuracy 43

Your Right To Make A Statement If Reinvestigation Does Not
Resolve The Dispute 43

Your Rights To Notify The World That A Disputed Item Is
Deleted Information Or That You Filed A Consumer Statement 43

Investigative Consumer Reports 44

Restrictions On Re-use Of Investigative Consumer Reports 44

Notification To Consumer Of Adverse Action Because Of Information
Obtained From A Person Other That A Consumer Reporting Agency 45

Your Right To Monetary Damages From A Consumer Reporting
Agency For Noncompliance With The Fair Credit Reporting Act 45

Penalty For Willful Noncompliance 45

Penalty For Negligent Noncompliance 46

No Action Exists For Defamation Or Invasion Of Privacy 46

Jurisdiction Of Courts 46

Relation To State Laws 47

Part VI - The Importance Of A Major Credit Card 48

How To Obtain A Major Credit Card 48

Part VII - For Women Only; Obtaining Credit In Your Own Name 49

How To Piggy Back On Your Joint Credit History To Get Your
Own Credit Card History 49

Part VIII - The Forms... 50

Government Statistics Indicate That Approximately One Out Of Every Four Americans Over The Age Of 18 Has A Potential Credit Problem.

- Are you one of the thousands upon thousands of Americans who are rejected for credit ?
- Are you frustrated and feel that you have nowhere to turn for advice or guidance ?
- Save seven hundred dollars or more on attorney's fees and credit repair clinics.
- The only self-help manual of its kind.
- **Challenge the credit giants that control your future.**
- Repairing a poor credit rating is an inevitable off-spring of the 'buy-now-pay-later' mentality of the 1980's.
- Better and cheaper than a credit repair clinic. Get prompt deletion of inaccurate, outdated or unverified negative information.
- End frustration.
- Correct your credit records within four (4) months.
- Easy to use, annotated legal forms professionally drafted by experts in the field will help.
- Do you want to fight back ?

Now You Can !

- Have you realized that credit is not a luxury but a necessity ?
- Get a major credit card by learning the secrets of the credit professionals.
- Do you want a borrowing capacity ?
- Do you want to be able to fulfill your dream of buying a house, buying a car, or investing in real estate ?
- Do you want a credit card regardless of credit history, job or income ?

Now You Can !

Bad Credit Histories Can Be Erased Or Rewritten!

Play David to the Goliaths of the credit reporting industry. Reading and understanding your rights under the law and following the easy to use FORMS in this book should help to clean up your poor credit record.

This manual attempts to help consumers restore good credit ratings.

Help exists even for those of you with judgments docketed against you. Little known trade secrets to help you are revealed for the first time by talented and dedicated professionals.

You Can Help Yourself

The Federal Fair Credit Reporting Act is a self-help act. It encourages a well-informed and self-motivated consumer vigilantly to protect and safeguard his rights.

The Consumer Reporting Agency is NOT your enemy. They only compile consumer reports based upon what sources **including you** tell them about you.

This self-help manual and the attached self-explanatory forms will enable you to contest, amend, supplement, erase and re-write your credit history. **You can improve your credit report**.

This Manual Is Better Than So-called Credit Repair Clinics

Hundreds of so-called credit repair clinics have sprung up in recent years. They advertise that they can remove unfavorable marks and clean up your credit report based upon loopholes in the Federal law.

These small businesses claim they can fix client's credit records, but at a cost of several hundred dollars or more.

One tactic normally used by credit clinics is to flood the credit bureaus with requests for verification of truthful derogatory information. A request which is not reverified within a reasonable time must be removed from your record under the Fair Credit Reporting Act.

Often these credit repair clinics cannot accomplish their goals. The credit reporting bureaus recognize the flooding technique and ignore the requests as "**frivolous and irrelevant disputes**" which need not be reverified under The Act.

Another credit bureau defensive tactic is to reverify the extraneous information in the repair clinic's request at a later time and then restore the derogatory information to your credit report.

The credit bureaus may also ignore the clinic's activities as third party communications to which the bureau need not respond under the Fair Credit Reporting Act. The credit reporting agencies cannot discuss your consumer report with unauthorized third parties.

The moral of the credit repair clinic story is NEVER rush the credit bureau with multiple requests at the same time.

TRW Inc., one credit giant, has sued at least one credit repair clinic for allegedly advising consumers to flood it with "frivolous" credit disputes.

Ostensibly, credit repair clinics are supposed to help consumers where credit records contain incorrect or outdated information. The clinics also appeal to people with bad credit histories who are looking to beat the system. This is why credit repair clinics often don't work. The credit reporting industry has smartened up and is taking affirmative action to defend against them. Credit bureaus don't like to be fooled and won't let credit repair clinics poison the stream of pure credit information.

You can't beat the system, but you can work **within the system to repair your credit**.

The explanatory text and forms in this manual are designed to anticipate and solve many common credit problems. The text and forms will provide the map through the minefield of credit repair.

The textual portion of the manual presents an overview of the credit system and how **your life is affected by the credit decisions made by other people.**

The forms are designed to help you communicate with your creditors and the credit reporting agencies in terms they understand and relate to. Each form is accompanied by easy fill-in- the blanks-instructions. Many of the forms are multifaceted and are designed to open a line of further communications by telephone.

Every case is different with its own special wrinkles and circumstances. However, the principles and forms contained in this manual judiciously utilized over time should help you to solve many common credit problems.

Take a moment to review the following list of forms. Note that the form number corresponds to the section of the Fair Credit Reporting Act dealing with the activity to which the form relates.

List Of Forms

FORM NAME	FORM I.D. NUMBER
Settlement Agreement	Creditor-1
Request for a Copy of Your Investigative Consumer Report	Form 606
Request for Deletion of Obsolete Information	Form 607
Request for Personal Interview with Consumer Reporting Agency	Form 610
Request for Telephone Interview with Consumer Reporting Agency	Form 610(b)(2)
Notice of Disputed Claim to Credit Reporting Agency	Form 611(a)
Consumer Statement	Form 611(b)
Your Request to the Consumer Reporting Agency to Furnish Notification of Deletion of Disputed Items or the Filing of a Consumer Statement - Made <u>Within</u> 30 Days After Notification of Adverse Credit Decision	Form 611(d)
Your Request to the Consumer Reporting Agency to Furnish Notification of Deletion of Disputed Items or the Filing of a Consumer Statement - Made <u>After</u> 30 Days From Notification of Adverse Credit Decision	Form 611(d)(2)
Consumer's Written Request for Reasons for Adverse Action	Form 615(b)
Letter to the Federal Trade Commission	Letter
Letter to State or County Consumer Protection Agency	Letter
Letter to Better Business Bureau	Letter
Complaint and Demand for a Jury Trial	Complaint
Bank Credit Application	First National Bank of Marin
Bank Disclosure Statement	First National Bank of Marin
Request to Consumer Reporting Agency to Verify New Data to be Added to your file	Supplemental-1
Obtaining Credit Files in Wife's Own Name	Equal Opportunity Credit Act Form-1
*Satisfaction of Judgment	Form Creditor-2
*Discontinuance of Action	Discontinuance
*Order Vacating Judgment	Form Creditor-3
IRS Offer in Compromise	IRS Form 656
Form of Taxpayer's Statement In Support of Offer In Compromise	Statement
IRS Statement of Financial Condition	IRS Form 433
*Order to Show Cause to Re-Open Default Judgment	Order

* These court forms may vary in appearance, format, and size from state to state. The content of the forms should be substantially correct. The author of this book is only licensed to practice in New York. Accordingly, it would be wise for you to consult with the Clerk of the Court or a local legal stationery store. **You may also be able to prevail upon the creditor and the creditor's attorney to prepare and file these forms**.

These forms will allow you to deal with:
1 - Credit Reporting Agencies
2 - Debt Collection Agencies
3 - Your Creditors

BEWARE OF CREDIT FRAUD

According to a recent *Wall Street Journal* article a new credit scam has been circulating. This swindle may affect you. Unscrupulous credit clinics obtain **your** name and **your** social security number and sell your credit credentials to another person possessing the same name.

Imagine your surprise when you discover that you are in default of several obligations incurred by a bogus you.

Using computers and stolen access codes "credit doctors" tap into credit bureau, bank and other data bases to extract information concerning names, loan histories, Social Security numbers and addresses of people with good credit histories. They then sell the information to clients with poor credit records to use when applying for credit.

The sad truth is that the scam works. All it takes is a similar name and a thief's ability to bribe his way into or crack creditors' computer access codes. This crime of the future (which is happening now) creates nightmares for the victims. Not only are innocent consumers surprised to find unauthorized and bogus purchases on their credit reports, but also merchants have been stuck with millions of dollars of fraudulent sales.

One innocent silver-haired art dealer, who had always paid her bills on time, was denied an oil company credit card because she had too many delinquent bills outstanding. To her panic her consumer report showed $40,000 in charges made in her name for items she had never ordered including a fur coat and a leased Mercedes-Benz.

A private detective traced the spending spree to an unemployed woman with a similar name, but twenty years younger than the art dealer and of a different race. The imposter had gotten the Social Security number and other credit data from a man who counseled poor people on repairing their credit.

According to newspaper reports the scam started in the city of Houston where purchases of almost $20,000,000 have been traced to phony credit data. The loot includes jewelry, television sets and vacations. An auto dealer sold 90 new cars to buyers with doctored credit, including eight members of the same family. Another woman bought at least five houses.

Credit bureaus deny that the problem is critical. They feel that rampant illegal access to their systems does not exist. The Big Three credit reporters (TRW, Equifax and Trans Union) claim to have invested heavily in security systems that flag unauthorized intrusions. They also purport to have made it more difficult for legitimate subscribers to browse through their files without authorization.

The success of the scams, however, indicate that technological safeguards aren't always foolproof. The schemes rely, in part, on business people greedy for sales, who overlook obvious frauds and even referred customers to credit doctors.

Authorities regard a 70 year old sometime Baptist preacher as the father of credit doctoring. With a $600 Tandy computer, access codes allegedly purchased from a credit bureau employee, and the alias of "Reverend", he took up one of the healing arts-- credit doctoring.

Through word of mouth, he had hundreds of clients who had lost their credit and were desperate to regain it. For fees that ranged up to $1500, the Reverend repaired their credit--sort of. He used the purloined access codes to retrieve the credit files of credit worthy people with names similar to his clients' names. The Reverend gave his client the information needed to successfully complete a new credit application.

According to the police who apprehended him, the Reverend said he wanted to undermine the credit granting process. The Reverend viewed credit as a form of slavery imposed on blacks by whites. He wanted to destroy the whole credit system.

His credit doctoring hit the credit system like an explosion. Every client became a walking time bomb, set to detonate as soon as the client stopped making payments. Banks, auto dealerships and retailers began racking up huge fraud losses. **Innocents whose credit histories were filched still live in terror of the dunning notices for things they didn't buy.**

One female victim said she felt like she had been raped when it first happened to her. Another woman had used the victim's name to buy a new Cadillac and a $35000 worth of home improvements. The victim's credit file now has a notice to lenders that she had been victimized by credit fraud.

Perhaps the most bizarre instance involved a college student living alone in a one bedroom apartment who received a past due notice for a $500 electric bill. After checking she discovered that the imposter not only stiffed the electric company, but also filed a bankruptcy petition using her name and Social Security number. The petition for bankruptcy listed over $100,000 in unpaid bills.

Investigators for the credit bureau traced the bankruptcy petition and other frauds to a member of the Reverend's congregation. She pleaded no contest to a charge of theft and has been sentenced to ten years' probation and is expected to testify against the credit doctor for whom she worked. She says, "I am not a criminal. My security is not down here."

Pointing with a dramatic sweep at the sky she said, "My security is up there!"

The Reverend has pleaded guilty in Federal court to fifteen charges of possessing unauthorized access codes with intent to defraud and was sentenced to an eight month prison term.

Beware Of Innocent Errors

A friend of the author was denied credit when an innocent entry on her credit report was misinterpreted by credit grantors.

She had become disgusted with VISA over a billing dispute. She resolved the dispute in her own mind by paying the VISA card bill and returning the VISA card as worthless. She cut the card in half and returned the severed halves to the VISA card issuer.

She was subsequently denied credit by other credit grantors. To her chagrin she discovered upon examination that credit had been denied because an entry on her consumer report indicated that she "had no credit with VISA". The reason she had no credit with VISA, of course, was because she had returned her credit card.

Innocent errors and misinterpretations of the truth can result in real credit problems. **Read and understand your consumer report, you and only you know all the facts and can correct innocent misstatements**.

An Overview Of The Organizational Structure Of This Manual

This manual is divided into several parts.

Part I concerns **credit** and **you** and explains the importance of credit and the information in your consumer credit file maintained by various credit reporting agencies.

Part II is an overview of the credit system framework.

Part III is an overview of your rights under the Fair Credit Reporting Act.

Part IV tells you how to help yourself and how to interface (a fancy word meaning deal with) your creditors and credit reporting agencies.

Part V is a detailed discussion of the finer points of the Fair Credit Reporting Act. This part sets out tedious but necessary background information which you may need or want to know. Part V begins with the entire text of the Fair Credit Reporting Act for those purists who want to read the original statutory language.

Part VI tells you how to order a major credit card.

Part VII is for women only to show them how to obtain a credit history and bank credit card in their own names.

Part VIII contains the FORMS.

Part 1 - Credit And You
The Importance Of Credit

What Is Credit?

Credit comes from the Latin *credito* meaning 'I believe...', i.e. I believe the borrower will pay. It has the same root as the word credence.

Credit, like the natural law of gravity, is the glue which binds the concrete of western civilization. Credit is extended whenever goods are sold or services rendered in advance of immediate cash payment.

With good credit you can buy now and pay later.

No credit or poor credit is an impediment similar to a physical handicap.

Before creditors lend money or merchants sell goods and services, they want to be certain that they will be paid back.

Since most creditors do not know you, they rely on compilations of your previous financial history in order to see if you have managed credit responsibly in the past and determine whether you are likely to be reliable now.

The Importance Of Your Credit File

Obviously, it is impossible for each creditor or merchant to verify each piece of financial information about each and every debtor or sale, so creditor-merchants turn to credit reporting agencies known as credit bureaus to provide an up to date credit file on you.

Your credit file is much more important than you realize. It is used by creditors (banks and merchants) to check, verify and evaluate your applications for credit. Your credit file is used by insurance companies to determine whether you are a risk they want to underwrite by extending insurance coverage to you.

Most importantly, your credit file can influence the **cost** of a loan or premium for insurance. Prime loans at bank's lowest price (interest rate) are reserved for the bank's best customers and minimal credit risks. The **worse** your credit picture looks, the **more** you must reward the creditor with higher rates in order to grant you credit or underwrite insurance coverage for you. Remember, that most loans are keyed to the mythical 'prime rate' because 'prime' is the bank's standard unit of measure to rate credit worthiness.

Your credit file may also be used by employers in making hiring decisions.

What Information Is Stored In Your Credit File

Credit bureaus compile the following information about you:
- Personal Statistics (consumer identification information)
- Account Information; and
- Public Records

A summary discussion of each follows.

Personal Statistics - consists of individual consumer information to identify you from the rest of the world.

(a) Your name - and title including past (maiden name), present name and aliases. Titles such as Jr., Senior, III and common names and common addresses present a constant potential for intermingling another person's adverse credit information on your report.

If you have a common name or live in the same house or apartment complex or even street with relatives having the same last name, your file may contain information about someone else.

(b) Your address - including past and present addresses for the past five years.

(c) Your Social Security number - This is your own number and no other Social Security number should appear on your records.

Slippery debtors often juggle a number on their Social Security number or credit application in a misguided effort to elude creditors. All that happens, however, is that credit will be declined if your Social Security number is not in order.

(d) Place of business - Your employment will be listed by name, address of employer, and the date employment was last reported to the credit bureau.

8

Other information such as salary or job tenure will only show if your employer reports such information and your particular agency desires to list it.

(e) Year of birth - Your year of birth.

When dealing with creditors on credit applications, do not misstate the facts concerning your name, address, social security number and date of birth.

These vital statistics are already in your credit file and deceiving a creditor makes you an instant loser in the hunt for credit.

The above mentioned consumer identifying information is, and should be, unique and singular to you. **No other person** should have your name, address, date of birth, Social Security number and employment history. Even twins have different Social Security numbers.

When you read your credit file for errors, verify that you are not being confused with someone else.

Account information - Consists of ledger information collected from subscribing creditors by the credit bureau.

1 - Name of Creditor
2 - Type of Creditor
3 - Account Number
4 - Account Information (if current, and balance)
5 - Number of late payments (one late payment per 30 day billing cycle)
6 - Charges you are disputing - you cannot be carried late when an account is in dispute.
7 - Accounts that were sent for collection.

The above information is in coded format and may be difficult to interpret. The key or glossary is on a separate sheet of paper and may be obtained from the agency issuing your consumer report. **Ask for the key to abbreviations.**

Remember that a 'c' is good. 'C' means current account, current payment.

Public records - Information culled from public records is usually maintained in the Office of the County Clerk.

1- Marriage
2- Divorce
3 - Judgments
4 - Tax Liens
5 - Arrests
6 - Convictions
7 - Lawsuits against you

As you can see, a great deal of information is contained in your credit profile. The Fair Credit Reporting Act assures that you can obtain a copy of your report, read it, and change it, if, as and when, necessary.

Remember information contained in your credit report is abbreviated with a coded and sometimes individually formatted system by each credit bureau. **A credit report may be difficult for the average consumer to understand.**

Examine the key to the code or glossary of your consumer report. You must understand every piece of information about you in order to find incorrect or negative or derogatory information in your files.

See the sample TRW credit profile and report of codes. If necessary, visit your credit bureau. See the discussion later in this manual on personal visits to your agency.

Your credit information is transmitted between the credit reporting agencies and the credit grantor-users by means of your consumer report. See the discussion later in this manual.

Part II - The Credit System Framework

Before you can improve your credit, you must understand how the credit reporting industry works. The following chapter is a short introduction to the credit system framework.

The Need For Credit Information

Creditors, credit grantors, retail merchants, banks, finance companies, landlords, employers, and just about everyone with a legitimate business purpose wants and needs good, current credit information about you.

Credit Reporting Agencies

Credit Reporting Agencies known in the trade as credit bureaus, and under the Federal Fair Credit Reporting Act as Consumer Reporting Agencies, solicit and compile ledger information about you from every possible credit grantor source including banks, finance companies, auto dealers, department stores, credit card issuers and other available credit generators. In this book the trade term "Credit Reporting Agency" and the statutory name "Consumer Reporting Agency" are used interchangably.

Credit bureaus provide information about how you have handled your current and previous credit extensions in a factual, non-judgmental format. Credit Bureaus are normally not biased toward either the creditor or the debtor. They are merely a storehouse of vital credit information which creditor-merchants need in order to make business decisions. Creditor-merchants want correct information upon which to make informed business decisions.

The agency's customers are: (a) other creditors who buy the compilation about you prior to extending or rejecting credit to you as their customer; and (b) **you**, because for a nominal fee, the Credit Reporting Agency will include information you wish to publish in their file concerning you.

Different Credit Reporting Agencies prepare different types of credit reports formatted with different information in different places. For example, consumer reports for mortgage lending purposes will have annual income (culled from the mortgage application you have filled out with your lender).

Part III - Overview Of The Fair Credit Reporting Act

Most credit grantors and vendors obtain a current copy of your consumer report from a credit reporting agency before approving your application for an extension of credit.

In most cases credit is granted and you don't receive notice of the issuance of the consumer report on you. If credit or insurance is denied or rejected, in whole or in part, or the cost of credit or insurance is increased based on unfavorable information from your credit report, the credit grantor-user or the credit reporting agency **must** notify you of that fact and provide the name and address of the credit reporting agency.

Where Do Credit Reporting Agencies Get Their Information?

Credit Reporting Agencies acquire their information from creditors who **subscribe** to their services and from **you.**

A credit file is opened on you when you first fill out a credit application with a creditor that requests a copy of your file from a credit reporting agency. Your personal statistics become a part of your initial file.

Information contained in each new credit application you sign for a potential extender of credit is entered into your file.

Certain large creditors such as banks, credit card issuers, large department stores and national vendors are subscribing creditors who supply credit reporting agencies with a detailed monthly account status generated and transmitted by computer tape.

How Accurate Is Your Credit File?

A mountain of accumulating information is sent every month from subscriber's computers to credit bureau computers.

While credit bureaus purport to have adequate checks and balances to screen incoming information from subscribers, they have no time or inclination to check every individual consumer's report to insure that your consumer report is accurate.

It is up to you to make sure that the information in your credit file is accurate !

Credit bureaus have no time or impetus to make every file complete. The file on you is probably not complete. You probably have a car loan, lease financing for an auto, a gasoline credit card and credit cards among other items which are not in your credit history.

Remember, all creditors do not subscribe to every credit bureau. Accordingly, your file will not necessarily be complete in every credit reporting agency.

For a small fee, most credit bureaus allow you to add this supplemental information to your file. See form **Supplemental-1**

It will take perseverance to correct your credit file in every credit bureau which may have a file about you. One easy way to locate the major credit bureaus in your area is to call your local bank lenders and department store credit managers and ask which credit bureaus they subscribe to, the location and telephone number of each.

The Consumer Report

The credit information about you is transmitted between the Credit Reporting Agencies and the credit grantor-users by means of a **consumer report,** informally called a "credit report".

The purpose of this manual is to enable you to obtain a copy of your consumer report with a view toward erasing, updating or revising unfavorable information contained in it, or supplementing favorable new information which you believe may help you.

What To Do When You Receive Notice Of Rejection Of Credit

If you have received a notification of rejection of credit within the past thirty (30) days, you are entitled to a **free** copy of your credit report from the issuing credit reporting agency.

Your rights stem from Section 615 of the Fair Credit Reporting Act. Section 615 is the trigger for all of your rights under the Fair Credit Reporting Act. Whenever you are denied credit, insurance or employment, or the rate for the credit is increased either wholly or in part because of information in a consumer report, the user of the information **must advise** you of the **adverse decision** and **must** supply the name and address of the credit reporting agency making the report. **This enables you to refute, update and dispute inaccurate or obsolete information and to otherwise tell your side of the story.**

The creditor-user may notify you orally or in writing. We believe most users respond in writing with a pre-printed form.

Whenever you receive a notice of credit rejection or other adverse credit decision, use this manual to order your free copy of your credit report. Then see what can be done to protect your rights.

A Note On Perseverance

An old baseball adage says: "If you don't succeed at first, try the outfield." Perseverance has helped many sports careers and perseverance will help your credit standing.

Motivated follow-up is important to verify that **your changes to your credit report have been made by creditors and credit reporting agencies.** Don't hesitate to call your creditor or credit reporting agency to insure that your changes have been accomplished.

If necessary, order a fresh copy of your consumer report.

If you don't succeed at first, try, try again. Papers get lost and computer entries can be mis-coded. So always check-up on your credit health.

Persistence pays off. Don't be afraid to be very persistent in your attempts to correct your credit report. Send all letters by **certified mail return receipt requested.**

The signed green receipt will be delivered to you by the post office within two (2) weeks.

Staple the signed return receipt card to your file copy of your letter. This is your proof of delivery.

If you do not receive a response within thirty (30) days, send a photocopy of your past communication and the signed receipt to the consumer reporting agency attention, General Manager. Tell them that in accordance with the Fair Credit Reporting Act, you expect an immediate and favorable response.

You must correct your consumer file at all credit bureaus used by your creditor. Credit bureaus do not notify each other of corrections to your consumer report.

Ask your creditor to identify all credit bureaus to which it reported the original mistake.

How To Add New Data To Your Consumer Report

Some credit bureaus will allow you to add additional credit information to your file concerning credit transactions with creditors who do not subscribe to that agency.

There are no negatives to adding good credit information to your consumer report. Favorable credit information is like chicken soup. It can't hurt. You never know what data will influence a creditor to grant credit to you. See form Supplemental-1 Request to Consumer Reporting Agency to Verify New Data to be Added to Your Credit File.

How Long Can Negative Adverse Information Remain On Your Consumer Report?

Negative information can be legally reported on your credit report for seven years.

Bankruptcies may remain part of your personal record for ten (10) years.

Chapter 13 cases more commonly known as Adjustment of Debts of an Individual with Regular Income, remain on your record for seven years.

Tax liens remain for seven years after they have been paid in full.

Unpaid tax liens may remain open indefinitely because The Fair Credit Reporting Act specifies no time limit for deleting unpaid tax liens.

Unpaid bills may remain for seven years.

Lawsuits may remain on your record for seven years or until the statute of limitations has expired. However, under regulations promulgated by Associated Credit Bureaus, Inc. (their trade group), bureaus should only report lawsuits for two (2) years unless disposition has been determined or the case is still known to be pending.

Civil judgments may remain on your credit record for seven years or until the statute of limitations has expired, whichever is longer. Civil Judgments normally have a ten (10) year statute of limitations and may be renewed for a further ten (10) year period. This will vary from state to state.

Accounts placed on collection may remain on your credit report for seven years from the date of charge-off.

Charged-off accounts may remain on your consumer report for seven years from the date of charge-off.

Records of arrest or indictment may remain on your credit record for seven years. **If the criminal case was dismissed or the consumer found not guilty, the arrest or indictment or criminal proceeding should no longer be listed in a consumer report.**

Record of conviction of a crime may remain on your credit report for seven years from the date of disposition, parole or release.

Late payment records may remain on your report for seven years.

Miscellaneous adverse items may remain on your report for seven years.

Favorable or neutral data may remain indefinitely as no time limitation mandates its removal.

Exceptions: the duty to delete unfavorable or derogatory information after seven years does not apply to:

(a) Credit transactions involving a principal amount of $ 50,000 or more, and
(b) Employment information relating to a job at an annual salary which equals or exceeds $ 20,000.

How To Remove Accurate But Negative Information From Your Credit Report

You attempt to remove accurate but negative information from your credit report in the same manner as porcupines make love, very delicately.

Removal of derogatory information is a sensitive and difficult operation requiring the acquiescence, if not consent of your creditor.

You must enlist the active support of the credit manager of the creditor. Explain the extenuating circumstances and other reasons behind the adverse information and ask the credit manager to advise the credit reporting agency that the adverse information about you is no longer verifiable. Unverifiable adverse information must be dropped from your credit report.

Credit managers tend to be cynical, sarcastic, hard nosed people. The reason is that they hear dead-beat sob-stories every hour, every day and they are used to a history of broken promises and betrayals. If you ever need open heart surgery, you want to reserve a credit manager's heart because it's still in the original packing crate and has never been used.

Credit managers have one fatal flaw. They love to collect money and melt at the prospect of "fresh blood" funds being collected on old dead accounts. Ply credit managers with money in exchange for their promise to help you delete unfavorable information from your credit report.

Never break a promise to a credit manager. Each promise of payment is logged onto a computerized history record.

Remember to get the credit manager's written agreement in Form Creditor 1 or otherwise to report to the credit bureau that the adverse information on your account is no longer verifiable and must be deleted from your credit file.

How To Find Your Credit Reporting Agency

In addition to the three major nationwide consumer reporting agencies listed below, there is usually a local consumer reporting agency based in your community, county or similar political subdivision.

The Big Three Major National Consumer Reporting Agencies

- TRW Credit Information Service
  505 City Park West
  Orange, CA. 92667
  (714) 991-5100

- Trans Union Credit Information
  444 No. Michigan Avenue
  Chicago, Illinois 60611

- CBI/EQUIFAX
  P.O. Box 4091
  Atlanta, Georgia 30302
  (404) 329-1725

Directory of Credit Bureau offices

The following company maintains a directory of Credit Bureau Offices:

- BANKCARD HOLDERS OF AMERICA
  650 Herndon Parkway, Suite 120
  Herndon, Virginia 22070
  (703) 481-1110

They purport to be a non-profit organization helping bankcard holders to become informed consumers, and for a modest fee, may be able to locate your credit bureau if all else fails.

Many credit reporting agencies are affiliated with the BIG THREE data bases. There are however, independent local agencies.

Finding your local consumer reporting agency

Look in the telephone directory (yellow pages) under 'Credit Reporting Agencies' or 'Consumer Reporting Agencies' and obtain their mailing address and telephone number. Use the list below to locate the credit bureau nearest to you, which will be the one most likely to maintain your complete file.

NORTHEASTERN REGION CREDIT BUREAUS

CONNECTICUT
BRIDGEPORT, CT. CBI, 2505 MAIN ST., SUITE 229, STRATFORD, CT 06497. 203/377-5478
BRIDGEPORT, CT 06604. TRW BRIDGEPORT, 2 LAFAYETTE SQ., 350 FAIRFIELD AVE., SUITE 301. 203/579-7857
HARTFORD, CT. TRW HARTFORD AREA, 350 FAIRFIELD AVE., BRIDGEPORT, CT 06604. 203/335-9663
NEW HAVEN, CT 06511. CREDIT BUREAU OF CONNECTICUT (TRANSUNION), P.O. BOX 1801, 414 CHAPEL STREET. 203/776-1733
NEW LONDON, CT 06320. CBI NEW LONDON, 61 BANK STREET. 203/443-8941.
STATEWIDE: CBI CONNECTICUT, 500 BI-COUNTY BLVD., SUITE D4, FARMINGDALE, NY 11735. 516/845-1247

DELWARE:
WILMINGTON, DE. BANK CREDIT BUREAU (TRANSUNION), P.O. BOX 320, PHILADELPHIA, PA 19105. 302/239-8800.

DISTRICT OF COLUMBIA:
WASHINGTON, D.C. 20013. CBI WASHINGTON, D.C., P.O. BOX 1617. 301/680-0770.

MAINE:
STATEWIDE: TRW, 350 FAIRFIELD AVE., BRIDGEPORT, CT 06604. 207/772-3771.

MARYLAND:
BALTIMORE, MD 21203. CBI - BALTIMORE, P.O. BOX 926, BALTIMORE, MD 21203. 301/332-4600.
COLUMBIA, MD 21045. TRW, P.O. BOX 779. 301/381-3200.
SALISBURY, MD 21081. CREDIT BUREAU OF DEL-MAR-VA, 530 RIVERSIDE DR. 301/742-9551.
SILVER SPRING, MD. CBI -- WASHINGTON AREA, P.O. BOX 1617, WASHINGTON, D.C. 20013. 301/680-0770.
STATEWIDE: TRANSUNION-MID-ATLANTIC DIVISION, P.O. BOX 380R, PHILADELPHIA, PA 19107. 301/796-5234.

MASSACHUSETTS:
BOSTON, MA 02116. CREDIT BUREAU SERVICES, F6 ST. JAMES AVENUE, P.O. BOX 73. 617/357-5487
BROCKTON, MA 02403. CREDIT DATA OF NEW ENGLAND, P.O. BOX 1941, 10 CHRISTY'S DRIVE. 508/588-4422
WAKEFIELD, MA 01880. TRW - WAKEFIELD AREA, 16 LAKESIDE OFFICE PARK. 617/245-5150
WORCHESTER, MA 01608. CREDIT BUREAU SERVICES, 1115 MECHANICS TOWER. 617/756-1567.
STATEWIDE: TRANSUNION-NORTH EASTERN DIVISION, P.O. BOX 40, REGO PARK, NY 11374. 718/459-1800 OR 617/438-4589.

NEW HAMPSHIRE:
MANCHESTER, NH 03105. TRW, 55 BRIDGE ST., P.O. BOX 127. 603/624-2629.
STATEWIDE: TRANSUNION - NORTH EASTERN DIVISION, P.O. BOX 40, REGO PARK, NY 11374. 617/438-4589.

NEW JERSEY:
CAMDEN, NJ 08101. CREDIT BUREAU ASSOCIATES, 817 CARPENTER, P.O. BOX 203. 609/488-4900.
PARSIPPANY, NJ 07054. TRW, P.O. BOX 271, 5 CENTURY DRIVE. 201/285-4840.
REGO PARK, NY 11374. TRANSUNION - NEW JERSEY DIVISION, P.O. BOX 40. 718/459-18J0.
SHREWSBURY, NJ 07701. CBI NEW JERSEY, 628 SHREWSBURY AVENUE. 201/842-7500.
TINTON FALLS, NJ 07724. CBI TINTON FALLS, 766 SHREWSBURY AVENUE. 800/392-6807.
STATEWIDE: CREDIT DATA, 200 MERRIMAC STREET, BOSTON, MA 02114. 508/580-4800.

NEW YORK:
ALBANY, NY 12203. CBI ALBANY, 3 CORPORATE PLAZA, WASHINGTON AVE EXTENSION. 518/869-6699.
BUFFALO, NY 14202. TRW BUFFALO, 1000 CATHEDRAL PARK TOWER, 37 FRANKLIN STREET. 716/849-1288.
FARMINGDALE, NY 11735. CBI, 500 BI-COUNTY BLVD. 516/845-1249.
GENEVA, NY 14456. CREDIT BUREAU AFFILIATES, P.O. BOX 391, 34 SENECA STREET. 315/789-6600.
NEW YORK CITY: TRW, 5 CENTURY DRIVE, PARSIPPANY, NJ 07054. 212/233-8569.
REGO PARK, NY 11374. TRANSUNION - P.O. BOX 40. 718/459-1800.
ROCHESTER, NY 14604. TRW ROCHESTER, 1605 MARINE MIDLAND PLAZA, SUITE 1605. 716/546-6190.
SEAFORD, L.I., NY 11783. CBI - SEAFORD, 2234 JACKSON AVE., 2ND FL. 516/845-1198.
SYRACUSE, NY 13203. FACSDATA CREDIT BUREAU OF UPSTATE NEW YORK, 404 OAK STREET. 315/425-0915.

OHIO:

AKRON, OH 44313. CSC CREDIT BUREAU OF AKRON, 2641 W. MARKET STREET. 216/867-0780.
BLUE ASH, OH 45242. TRW CINCINNATI, 4445 LAKE FOREST DRIVE, SUITE 530. 513/563-8790.
CANTON, OH 44701. UNITED CREDIT BUREAU, 128 3RD STREET, NE, P.O. BOX 20740. 216/456-2731.
CHILLICOTHE, OH 45601. CREDIT BUREAU SERVICES OF SE OHIO, 155 S. WATT STREET, P.O. BOX 2080. 614/773-2181.
CINCINNATI, OH 45201. CREDIT BUREAU OF CINCINNATI, 309 VINE ST., P.O. BOX 1239. 513/651-6208.
CLEVELAND, OH 44101. TRANSUNION - NORTHEASTERN OHIO DIVISION, P.O. BOX 5882. 216/579-3948.
CLEVELAND AREA: CREDIT BUREAU OF MIDDLETOWN, P.O. BOX 8682, MIDDLETOWN, OH 45042. 513/423-9481.
COLUMBUS, OH 43215. CREDIT BUREAU OF COLUMBUS, 170 E. TOWN STREET, P.O. BOX 1838. 614/222-5327.
COLUMBUS, OH 43229. TRW COLUMBUS, 1105 SCHROCK ROAD, SUITE 822. 614/431-0032.
DAYTON, OH 45402. CSC CREDIT SERVICES OF DAYTON, P.O. BOX 878 MCS. ATTN: C1. 513/224-1005.
FINDLAY, OH 45402. HANCOCK CREDIT SERVICES, 118 E. SANDUSKY STREET. 419/422-5161.
KENTON, OH 43326. CREDIT BUREAU OF LOGAN/HARDIN COUNTY (TRANSUNION), 115 WEST FRANKLIN, P.O. BOX 201, 419/673-1275 (HARDIN COUNTY), 513/592-2230 (LOGAN COUNTY).
LIMA, OH 45802. CREDIT BUREAU OF LIMA (TRANSUNION), 121 W. HIGH STREET, SUITE 405, P.O. BOX 1847. 419/228-3121.
MANSFIELD, OH 44903. CREDIT BUREAU SERVICES, 1336 PARK AVE. WEST. 419/529-4405.
MARION, OH 43302. CREDIT BUREAU SERVICES, 170 E. COLUMBIA. 614/387-7000.
MIDDLEBURG HEIGHTS, OH 44130. TRW CLEVELAND, PLAZA SOUTH TWO, 7261 ENGLE RD., SUITE 310. 216/243-5330.
NEWARK, OH 43055. CREDIT BUREAU OF NEWARK, 141 W. MAIN STREET, P.O. BOX F. 614/345-6651.
SANDUSKY, OH 44870. NORTH CENTRAL OHIO CREDIT SERVICE (TRANSUNION), P.O. BOX 355, 809 FEICK BUILDING, 158 E. MARKET STREET. 419/625-4231.
SPRINGFIELD, OH 45504. CREDIT BUREAU OF SPRINGFIELD, 20 W. COLUMBIA STREET, P.O. BOX 1968. 513/323-4666.
TOLEDO, OH 43604. CREDIT BUREAU OF TOLEDO (TRANSUNION), 626 MADISON, ATTN: CONSUMER RELATIONS. 419/244-8211.
TOLEDO, OH 43615. TRW TOLEDO, 5577 AIRPORT HIGHWAY, SUITE 205. 419/531-8943.
WARREN, OH 44482. CREDIT BUREAU OF WARREN (TRANSUNION), P.O. BOX 1192, 473 SOUTH STREET. 216/394-4100.
YOUNGSTROWN, OH 44503. CREDIT REPORTING SERVICE (TRANSUNION), 275 FEDERAL PLAZA W., SUITE 902. 216/746-5028.
ZANESVILLE, OH 43701. CREDIT BUREAU OF ZANESVILLE, 1846 DRESDEN ROAD. 614/452-7525.
STATEWIDE: CSC CREDIT SERVICES (OH DIVISION), P.O. BOX 674422, HOUSTON, TX 77267. 1-800-392-7816.
STATEWIDE: TRANSUNION - OHIO DIVISION, 222 FIRST STREET, SUITE 201, LOUISVILLE, KY 40202. 502/584-0121.

PENNSYLVANIA:

ALLENTOWN, PA 18101. ASSOCIATED CREDIT BUREAU SERVICES, INC., P.O. BOX 1640, 739 HAMILTON MALL. 215/829-9200.
ERIE, PA 16512. CREDIT BUREAU OF LANCASTER COUNTY, P.O. BOX 1271, 2491 PAXTON ST. 717/293-9225.
PHILADELPHIA, PA 19106. CBI PHILADELPHIA, PUBLIC LEDGER BLDG., SUITE 1072, 6TH AND CHESTNUT STREETS. 215/923-1536.
PHILADELPHIA, PA 19107. TRANSUNION - PHILADELPHIA DIVISION, P.O. BOX 360. 215/496-6600.
PITTSBURGH, PA. TRANSUNION - PITTESBURGH DIVISION, P.O. BOX 390, PHILADELPHIA, PA 19105. 412/922-5298.
READING, PA 19603. CREDIT BUREAU OF READING & BERKS COUNTY, 135 S. 5TH ST., P.O. BOX 79. 215/375-4461.
SCRANTON, PA 16501. TRW SCRANTON, 420 CONNEL BUILDING, 717/344-7191.
WILLIAMSPORT, PA 17701. TAMMAC CREDIT SERVICES, 211 W. 4TH STREET. 717/326-0521.
YORK, PA 17401. CREDIT BUREAU OF YORK, 33 SOUTH DUKE STREET. 717/843-8685.

RHODE ISLAND:

PROVIDENCE, RI 02901. TRW PROVIDENCE AREA, 40 FOUNTAIN STREET, P.O. BOX 1366, 401/273-7500.
WARWICK, RI 02888. TRANSUNION, 231 ELM STREET. 401/781-7460.

VERMONT:

BURLINGTON, VT 05402. TRW BURLINGTON, P.O. BOX 56, 802/863-2589.

WEST VIRGINIA:

BECKLEY, WV 25801. CREDIT BUREAU OF BECKLEY, INC., 205 MCCREERY STREET. 304/252-6382.
CHARLESTON, WV 25326. CSC W. VIRGINIA CREDIT BUREAU REPORTING SERVICES, 8 CAPITOL STREET, 2ND FL., TERMINAL BLDG., P.O. BOX 1707. 304/343-6111.
CLARKSBURG, WV 26301. CREDIT BUREAU OF CLARKSBURG, P.O. BOX 1880, 120 S. SECOND STREET. 304/624-5623.
HUNTINGTON, WV 25701. CREDIT BUREAU OF HUNTINGTON, 1327 6TH AVENUE. 304/529-2461.
MARTINSBURG, WV 25401. CBI MARTINSBURG, 134 SOUTH QUEEN STREET, 2ND FLOOR, OR P.O. BOX 872. 304/263-3379.
PARKERSBURG, WV 26102. CENTRAL CREDIT BUREAU, P.O. BOX C, 325 6TH STREET. 304/485-4444.
WHEELING, WV 26003. TRANSUNION TRI-STATE CREDIT EXCHANGE, 901 MARKET STREET. 304/233-6330.
WILLIAMSON, WV 25661. BLACK DIAMOND CREDIT BUREAU, 730 REAR ALDERSON STREET, P.O. BOX 1782. 304/235-7929.
WILLIAMSON, WV 25661. CREDIT BUREAU OF WILLIAMSON, SECOND AVENUE & COURT STREET. 304/235-5252.

PUERTO RICO:

SAN JUAN, PUERTO RICO 00936. CBI SAN JUAN, 1590 PONCE DE LEON AVENUE, URB CARIBE, OR P.O. BOX 4983. 809/751-0291.

© 1990 Bankcard Holders of America. All rights reserved.

NOTE: THE ABOVE LIST SHOWS THE DIFFICULTY IN FINDING THE MAJOR CREDIT BUREAUS. THEY COVER LARGE TERRITORIES AND OFTEN LOCATE IN NEIGHBORING SUBURBS OF LARGE CITIES.

How To Obtain A Copy Of Your Consumer Report

Obtain a copy of your credit report from your national or local Credit Reporting Agency by using Forms **610 and 610(b)(2)**.

If you have received notification of rejection of credit within the past thirty (30) days, you are entitled to a **free copy** of your credit report. If you have not been denied credit within the last thirty (30) days, it would be a good idea to call your credit reporting agency and determine their fee for providing you with a copy of their consumer report about you.

You can expect to pay from five to thirty dollars. Local agencies charge from $8 (by State law in California) to a reasonable fee under the Federal Fair Debt Reporting Act. In no event is the fee to exceed the charge the agency charges their creditor-grantor customers for your report.

Remember, you are entitled to a **free copy** of your consumer report if you have been denied credit within the immediately preceding thirty (30) days.

How To Read Your Consumer Report

A TRW sample credit profile for John Q. Consumer is reproduced on the following page. The TRW Credit Profile Report Key is shown immediately following the sample report. Note the codes and shorthand used in both the TRW Credit Profile and the Credit Profile Report.

Note that the Credit Profile Report has numbers which are keyed to items on the Credit Profile. THE KEYED NUMBERS ARE NOT EASY TO FIND. LOOK CAREFULLY AND BE SURE YOU FIND AND UNDERSTAND THE CODES.

If you still have questions, ask your Credit Reporting Agency for clarification.

How to Read Your TRW Credit Report

1. Identifying information used to obtain this report from the TRW data base.
2. Identification number. Please include on all correspondence with us.
3. Your name and address as reported to us by one of your credit grantors on the date shown.
4. Your employer's name and address as last reported to us by one of your credit grantors when making an inquiry on the date shown. This information is not verified nor does the date indicate your date hired.
5. Your Social Security number as reported to us by one of your credit grantors.
6. These columns indicate positive, non-evaluated and negative status comments.
   Positive - The status is generally viewed as favorable by credit grantors.
   Negative - The status is generally viewed as unfavorable by credit grantors.
   Non-evaluated - The status may be viewed as favorable, unfavorable or neutral depending on each credit grantor's policy.
7. FACS+ service checks whether an SSN is valid, whether an address in non-residential and how many time the SSN and address have been used on inquiries during the past 120 days.
8. The method by which the credit grantor reports information.
   A - Information is primarily reported in an automated manner.
   M - Information is primarily reported in a manual manner.
9. The name of the reporting subscriber and its assigned TRW identification number.
10. Abbreviated code for the Equal Credit Opportunity Act (ECOA) account designation, which explains the legal relationship to the account. If you are no longer associated with the account, a termination code will appear. (Codes explained in ECOA Account Designation and Termination Codes section on next pages.)
11. Account number or court docket number.
12. Abbreviated description of the payment status of the account as of the date noted. (See Explanation of Status Comments on next pages.)
13. Date the account was opened. 5-Y or 10-Y indicates opened prior to five or ten years respectively.
14. Scheduled monthly payment amount. The amount may not be exactly what you paid when making your last reported payment.
15. Estimated monthly payment amount. The amount may not be exactly what you paid when making your last reported payment.
16. Date of the last payment you made which was reported to us.
17. Abbreviated description of the type of credit extended. (Abbreviations explained in Type of Account section on next pages.)
18. Time frames scheduled for account repayment. Charge accounts are stated as REV (revolving). All other accounts are stated in months with the exception of real estate types which are state in years.
19. Abbreviated explanation of amount of account. (See explanation under Amount Qualifier on next pages.) The dollar amount is represented in whole dollars. Public record items reflect the amount o debt filed in the court record rounded to the nearest $100. Amounts less than $100 are displayed as -$100.
20. Balance owing as of the date located to the immediate right.
21. Dollar amount past due, if any, as of the balance date.
22. Abbreviated code of the status of the account for each of the 24 months preceding the balance date (explained in 24-Month Payment Profile section o next pages). This information is read from left to right.
23. The name of a subscriber that has obtained a copy of your credit history on the date shown. May include type, terms and amount of credit applied for, if available.
24. Public record including court name, court code, docket number, type of public record, filing date, amount, judgment and creditor. This information may include bankruptcies, liens and/or judgments against you. The amount of debt filed in the court record is rounded to the nearest $100. Amounts less that $100 are displayed as - $100. Code defined in Public Records on next pages.
25. Profile report message. For further explanation, see Credit Profile Report Messages on next pages.

Updated CREDIT PROFILE Disclosure

TRW

Inquiry Information

(1) TCR2 DFD2 3499953 CONSUMER JOHN .S., 10655 B 91502,P-6613 S 92708, 235 E 14202, S-548603388,Y-1944,Z-ME,M-10655 BIRCH ST?BURBANK CA 91502,L-BIRCH

See comment below...Full identification information, including your Social Security Number is needed to check any disputed items.

IDENTIFICATION NUMBER

PAGE	DATE	TIME	PORT	N/V			
1	10-10-88	11:04:45	HP26	A60	CONSUMER	TCA1	56-005587/33 (2)

(3) 8-88 JOHN Q CONSUMER
10655 BIRCH ST
BURBANK CA 91502

(4) 4-88 AJAX HARDWARE
2035 BROADWAY
LOS ANGELES CA 90019

(5) SS# 548603388
YOB-1944

LINE NO.	Account Profile Pos Non Neg	Subscriber Name/Court Name / Status Comment / Status Date / Date Opened	Subscriber # Court Code / Type / Assn. Code Terms	Amount / Balance	Account/Docket Number / Balance Date / Amount Past Due	Payment Profile number of months prior to balance date 1 2 3 4 5 6 7 8 9 10 11 12
6						
7	> > >	FACS + SUMMARY (7)				
8						
9	> > >	PERSON ISSUED SS# IS DECEASED ON FACS FILE				
10						
11	> > >	FROM 06/01/88 NUMBER OF INQS WITH THIS SS# = 2				
12						
13	(8) A	MOUNTAIN BANK (9)	1139999 / 2 / ORIGL (10)		3562401973 (11)	
14		CURWAS30-3 2-88 9-85	SEC / 60 / $43000	$22227	9-26-88	C C C C C C C 1 C 1 C C
15			SCH MONTH PAY	$717	LASTPAY 8-88	C 1 C C C C C C C C C C
16						
17	A	HILLSIDE BANK (13)	3149999 / 5 / ORIGL		29144508119	
18		CUR ACCT 9-88 (12) 12-87	AUT / 48 / $6300	$5148	9-15-88	C C C C C - C C C
19		(14)	SCH MONTH PAY	$132	LAST PAY 8-88	
20						
21	A	HEMLOCKS	3319999 / 1 / HIBAL		986543184026	
22		CURR ACCT 10-88 8-88	CHG / REV / $600	$440	10-05-88	C C
23		(15)	EST MONTH PAY	$44		
24						
25	A	BAY COMPANY	3319999 / 1 / LIMIT		46812391013	
26		CUR WAS 60 4-88 10-Y	CHG / REV / $1500	$0	9-21-88	N N N N C 2 1 C C N N C
27			(17) (18)		LASTPAY 4-88 (16)	C C C 1 C N N N C 1 C C
28						
29	M	BOWERS	3369999 / 1 / C/OAM		221250	
30		CHARGE OFF 4-87 7-81	CHG / REV / $200			
31						
32	A	GARDEN FINANCE	3509999 / 1 / ORIGL		24187010 (20) (21)	
33		DELINQ 1209-88 3-87	UNS / 24 / $2200	$1400	9-17-88 / $425	3 2 1 C C C C C C C C C
34			EST MONTH PAY (19)	$100	LASTPAY 5-88	C C C C C C (22)
35						
36	A	WISTERIA FINANCE	3549999 / 4		5238610	
37		INQUIRY 11-18-87	AUT / 48 / $63000		(23)	
38						
39		CO SPR CT SANTA ANA	3019999		07505853 (24)	
40		JUDGMENT 10-19-86		$1200	ALLIED COMPANY	
41						
42	> > >	CHECKPOINT > > > > SS# IS 054860338/OTHER FILE IDENT: MID INIT IS Q				
43	1-88	JOHN Q CONSUMER				
44		6613 SADDLEBACK ROAD				
45		(25) ORANGE CA 92708				
46						
47		END -- TRW				

This disclosure is based on the identifying information supplied by you. If you did not supply us with your full name, addresses for the past 5 years, social security number and year of birth, this disclosure may not be complete.

Confidential See Reverse Side for Explanation & Instructions

Type of Account

ADD	Address information for mailing
AUT	Auto
A/M	Account monitored by credit grantor
BUS	Business
CCP	Combined credit plan
CHG	Charge account
CLS	Credit line secured
COL	Collection attorney
COM	Co-maker-not borrower
CPS	Consumer service Credentials
CRC	Credit card
CRD	Consumer relations display
C/C	Check credit or line of credit
DCP	Data correction profile
DCS	Debit counseling service
D/C	Debit card
EDU	Educational
EMP	Employment
FHA	FHA home improvement
F/C	FHA co-maker (not borrower)
F/S	Family support
GEA	Government employee advance
GFS	Government fee for service
GMD	Government miscellaneous debt
GOP	Government overpayment
G/B	Government benefit
G/F	Government fine
G/G	Government grant
H/E	Home equity
HHG	Secured by household goods and other collateral
H/I	Home improvement
H+O	Secured by household goods and other collateral
IDV	Address information for the government
INS	Insurance claims
ISC	Installment sales contract
I/L	Installment loan
LEA	Lease
MED	Medical debt
M/H	Mobile home
NCM	Note loan with co-maker
NTE	Note loan
PHC	Prescreen/extract report
PIA	Prescreen/invitation to apply
PMI	Prescreen/extract promotion inquiry
PPO	Prescreen/preapproved offer
PPI	Prescreen/post prescreen inquiry
PSC	Solicitation
P/S	Partially secured
QST	Account reviewed by credit grantor
RCK	Returned check
REC	Recreational merchandise
REN	Rental agreement
RVW	Account review by credit grantor
R/C	Conventional real estate mortgage-terms are in years
R/E	Real estate/specific type unknown-terms are in years
R/F	FHA real estate mortgage-terms are in years
R/O	Real estate mortgage with or without other collateral - usually a 2nd mortgage-terms are in years
R/V	VA real estate mortgage-terms are in years
SCO	Secured by a co-signer
SDL	Government secured direct loan
SEC	Secured
SGL	Government secured guaranteed loan
SUM	Summary of accounts with same status
UDL	Government unsecured direct loan
UGL	Government unsecured guaranteed loan
UNK	Unknown
UNS	Unsecured

Explanation of Status Comments

BK ADJ PLN	Debit included in or completed through Bankruptcy Chapter 13.
BK LIQ RE	Debit included in or discharged through Bankruptcy Chapter 7, 11 or 12.
CHARGE OFF	Unpaid balance reported as a loss by credit grantor
CLOS INAC	Closed inactive account
CLOS NP AA	Credit line closed; not paying as agreed.
COLL ACCT	Account seriously past due; account assigned to an attorney; collection agency or credit grantor's internal collection department.
CO NOW PAY	Now paying, was a charge-off
CR CD LOST	Credit card lost or stolen.
CR LN CLOS	Credit line closed; reason unknown or by consumer request; there may be a balance due.
CR LN RNST	Account now available for use and is in good standing; was a closed account.
CURR ACCT	This is either an open or closed account in good standing. If a credit card or charge account, it should be available for use and there may be a balance due. If account is closed, there were no past due amounts reported and it was paid.
CUR WAS COL	Current account; was collection account, insurance claim or government claim.
CUR WAS DL	Current account; was past due.
CUR WAS FOR	Current account; foreclosure was started.
CUR WAS 30 (etc.)	Current account; was past due the number of days indicated. The account has been current since the status date.
CUR WAS 30-2(etc.)	Current account; was past due the number of days indicated, the number of times indicated. Has been current since the status date.
DECEASED	Consumer reported as deceased.
DEED IN LIEU	Credit grantor received deed for collateral in lieu of foreclosure on a defaulted mortgage.
DELINQ 60(etc.)	Account past due date the number of days indicated.
DEL WAS 90	Account was delinquent 90 days past due date, now 30 or 60 days delinquent.
DEL WAS 120	Account was delinquent 120 days past due date, now 30, 60 or 90 days delinquent.
GOVCLAIM	Claim filed with government for insured portion of balance on defaulted student loan
FORECLOSURE	Credit grantor sold collateral to settle defaulted mortgage.
FORE PROC	Foreclosure proceeding started.
INQUIRY	A copy of the credit report has been sent to this credit grantor at their request.
INS CLAIM	Claim filed for payment of insured portion of balance on account secured by real estate.
NOT PAY AA	Account not being paid as agreed.
PAID ACCT	Closed account; zero balance; not rated by credit grantor.
PAID SATIS	Closed account; paid satisfactorily.
PD BY DLER	Credit grantor paid by the company which originally sold the merchandise.
PD CHG OFF	Paid account; was a charge-off.
PD COLL AC	Paid account; was a collection account, insurance claim or government claim.
PD FORECLO	Paid account; a foreclosure was started.
PD NOT AA	Paid account; some payments were made past the agreed due dates.
PD REPO	Paid account; was a repossession.
PD VOL SUR	Paid account; was a voluntary surrender.
PAID WAS 30(etc.)	Paid account; was past due the number of days indicated.
PAID WAS 30-2(etc.)	Paid account; was past due the number of days indicated, the number of times indicated.
REDMD REPO	Acount was a repossession; now redeemed.
REFINANCED	Account renewed or refinanced.
REPO	Merchandise taken back by credit grantor; there may be a balance due.
SCNL	Credit grantor cannot locate consumer.
SCNL NWLOC	Credit grantor could not locate consumer; consumer now located.
SETTLED	Account legally paid in full for less than the full balance.
TERM DFALT	Early termination by default of original terms of lease or sales contract.
TRANSFERRED	Account transferred to another office.
VOLUN SURR	Voluntary surrender.
30 DAY DEL	Account past due date 30 days.
30 2 TIMES (etc.)	Account past due date 30 days number of times indicated.
30 WAS 60	Account was delinquent 60 days past due date; now 30 days.

ECOA Account Designation and Termination Codes

0:	UNDESIGNATED	Accounts reported prior to November 1977.
1:	INDIVDUAL	This is the only person associated with this account. (Termination code H appears if mortgage loan was assumed by others.)
2:	JOINT/ CONTRACTUAL	This individual is expressly obligated to repay all debts on this account by reason of having signed an agreement to that effect. There are others associated with this account who may also have contractual responsibility. (Termination code B appears if association is terminated.)
3:	JOINT/ AUTHORIZED USER	This individual has use of this joint account for which another individual has contractual responsibility. (Termination code C appears if association is terminated.)
4:	JOINT/ UNDESIGNATED	This individual has use of this account. The association cannot be distinguished between 2 or 3 above. (Termination code D appears if association is terminated.)
5:	CO-MAKER	This individual has guaranteed this account and assumes responsibility should the maker default. (Termination code E appears if association is terminated.) This code only to be used in conjunction with code 7 maker (below).
6:	ON BEHALF OF	This individual has signed an application for the purpose of securing credit for another individual, other than spouse. (Termination code F appears if association is terminated.)
7:	MAKER	This individual is responsible for this account which is guaranteed by a co-maker. (Termination code G appears if association is terminated.) To be used in lieu of codes 2 and 3 when there is a code 5 co-maker.
X:	DECEASED	This individual has been reported as deceased. There may be other people associated with this account.

Amount Qualifier

ORIGL	Original amount of loan
LIMIT	Credit limit amount
HIBAL	Historically, the highest balance reported
UNKWN	Amount unspecified by credit grantor
C/OAM	Charge-off amount

24-Month Payment Profile

C	Current	6	180 days past due date
1	30 days past due date	-	No history reported for that month
2	60 days past due date		
3	90 days past due date	Blank	No history maintained
4	120 days past due date	N	Current/zero balance reported
5	150 days past due date		

Public Records

BK 7,11,12,13 FILE	Voluntary or involuntary petition in Bankruptcy Chapter 7,11; Chapter 12 Adjustment of Debt-Family; or Petition in Bankruptcy Chapter 13 filed.
BK 7,11,12 DISC	Voluntary or involuntary petition in Bankruptcy Chapter 7,11,discharged; or Chapter 12 discharged after completion.
BK 7,11,12,13 DISM	Voluntary or involuntary petition in Bankruptcy Chapter 7,11; or petition in Bankruptcy Chapter 12 or 13 dismissed.
BK 13-COMP	Petition in Bankruptcy Chapter 13 (adjustment of debt) completed.
JUDGMENT	Judgment.
JUDGMT SAT	Judgment satisfied (paid).
JUDG SAT VAC	Judgment vacated either before or after being satisfied.
NT RESPON	Not responsible notice (e.g., husband or wife claims not responsible for debts incurred by spouse).
TX LN	Tax lien - city, county, state, federal or mechanics lien.
TX REL	Tax lien released - city, county, state, federal or mechanics lien released.
SUIT	Suit.
SUIT DISMD	Suit dismissed or discontinued.
WAGE ASIGN	Wage assignment.
W/A RELEASE	Wage assignment released.

Part IV - How To Deal With Creditors

How To Deal Directly With Your General Creditors

1 - You can deal directly with your creditor. Call your creditor's main telephone number and ask for the Credit Manager.
2 - Many creditors have data banks which can only hold data for a few years.
3 - Specific data on customer complaints, and miscellaneous ledger information on old and unpaid accounts is often purged from the creditor's data bank within two (2) years to make room for new information concerning live accounts.

Most computer data bases are constantly balancing available computer memory against the amount of new data to be stored and the expense of increasing the system to hold new information. This balance is normally resolved by deleting or purging old dormant accounts including yours.

4   New payments on old written-off accounts are found money to a credit manager because the collection is from a source outside of the collection base. Your new payment is like an inheritance that the credit manager adds to the collection totals. Credit Managers will often make deals for a lesser sum in full settlement of the old claim of the creditor.
5 - The percentage of recoveries is the Credit Manager's report card. The percentage of recovery is a fraction: % of recovery = dollars collected/total bad debt

Your new found dollars collected increase the numerator of the fraction and increase the percentage of recovery.
6 - After you have settled an old case with the credit manager for a specific dollar amount, try to get a deferred payment plan so that you can pay the **new reduced** amount **over time.**
7 - Try to spread the deferred payments over twelve (12) equal installments.
8 - Depending on the amount owed and your other debts and expenses, many credit managers will authorize a twenty-four (24) month equal installment payment plan.
9 - After you have negotiated the reduced amount and the installment payment plan, ask the credit manager to update your credit report with the credit reporting agency to reflect that the adverse information is no longer verifiable.

Form Creditor 1 is a form of agreement of settlement that sets forth:
1 - The reduced amount owed by you.
2 - The installment payment terms.
3 - The creditor's agreement to notify any credit reporting agency to delete from your credit report adverse information which is no longer verifiable.
10 - Even if the creditor has obtained a judgment against you, it may be possible to have a friend or your spouse buy back or satisfy the judgment at a discount.

In either event, you or the creditor should file a Satisfaction of Judgment. See Form Creditor 2 - Satisfaction of Judgment.
11 - Even better, get the creditor to agree to Form Creditor 3, which is **an order to vacate judgment**. Vacating a judgment totally removes it from your credit record because the effect of such an agreement is to blot out the judgment as if it never existed.

An analogy that comes to mind is that vacating a judgment is like annulling a marriage. You don't need a divorce with an annulment because the marriage never existed. Likewise, vacating a judgment means that the judgment **never existed.**

How To Deal With Judgment Creditors

Judgments are particularly dangerous adverse information on your credit report because judgments result from a case in which you had owed money and antagonized a creditor to a point where the creditor was forced to sue you.

When a judgment has been entered, you owe additional court costs and interest. Furthermore, a final, binding and non-reversible public record of your debt exists and will exist for ten (10) years from the date of entry and may be renewed for another ten

(10) years in most states. In other words, you have no high cards left to play with in negotiating with your creditor; **except fresh money from a third party source.**

To remove a judgment from your credit file, you need the consent of your creditor.

Explain to your creditor that a third party friend or relative is willing to lend you money to pay the creditor, if the creditor agrees to vacate the judgment or assign all of the creditor's rights to your third party benefactor (who will then vacate the judgment).

The money must come from THIRD PARTY fresh blood sources because any money or property you have already belongs to your creditor by virtue of the judgment lien.

Notwithstanding the enhanced strength judgment creditors possess, many are willing to sell, vacate or discharge a judgment for less than the original debt or will agree to compromise court costs and interest. The reason is that the judgment creditor has been frustrated by exhausting all of his legal rights and still remains unsatisfied. Most judgment creditors cannot resist the deceptively compelling call of new fresh money from a non-obligated source in order to satisfy their original judgment. See the form on How to Vacate a Judgment.

How To Handle Tax Liens

Liens for unpaid taxes can be filed by the Federal and State governments and political subdivisions of the County and City governments. While most tax liens are for unpaid income or withholding taxes, political subdivisions of State governments can file tax liens against your real property for unpaid real estate taxes, sewer rents and other local assessments. Most liens against real estate are difficult to compromise because a savvy creditor knows that he will be paid when the real estate is eventually sold.

Federal and State bureaucracies are difficult to deal with. The advent of computerized files means that tax disputes often move themselves by computer programming into the assessment of a tax lien before you can ever speak to a human being. Your correspondence criss-crosses in the mails with ever ascending nasty computer letters from the tax authorities until a tax lien results.

State & Local Tax Liens

It is virtually impossible to compromise a State tax lien. The dollar amount of the lien is normally relatively low and State officials have little incentive to settle their claims. Perhaps they have no goals or objectives to meet or perhaps they just get paid the same at the end of the month whether they produce revenue or not. Sometimes it appears that they don't even care if they collect on the tax lien.

There can be three parts to a tax lien:
1 - Unpaid Taxes
2 - Interest on Unpaid Taxes
3 - Penalties

Collection and compromise policy will vary from State to State. This manual will not attempt to advise on the tax lien compromise policy of each state government. Suffice it to say that you should speak to a living person and try to negotiate:

1 - A Compromise
2 - A Payment Plan
3 - A Waiver of Interest or Penalties
4 - A letter to the Consumer Reporting Agency that the tax lien was filed in error and should be deleted from your credit report.

State officials may have limited authority to compromise interest and penalties.

Also, be alert for tax amnesty programs. Under most tax amnesty programs, the taxing authority is willing to waive interest and penalties in exchange for payment of the original tax due.

Federal Taxes

As a rule, the Internal Revenue Service is more pleasant to deal with than State Tax Agencies.

Everyone has a private horror story about the IRS. One favorite is a case where the IRS refused to believe that a person who owed them $150,000 really died and opened his grave to examine the dead body. In reality, Federal IRS employees are knowledgeable, helpful and understanding of taxpayer problems. After all, they live with these problems every day.

The IRS is so large, and its files so voluminous, that you will be nothing more than paperwork on a desk until you meet the ultimate human decision maker.

It is possible to compromise your tax liability with the IRS

Section 7122 of the Internal Revenue Code and Internal Revenue Service Form 656 deal with offers in compromise.

Because of the importance of this little known provision, the IRS instructions relating to form 656, are set forth below: (The entire form 656, Offers In Compromise, is included in the Forms part of this manual along with the companion IRS form 433 Statement Of Financial Condition And Other Information.)

Offer in Compromise - Form 656

Background

Section 7122 of the Internal Revenue Code provides that the Secretary may compromise any civil or criminal case arising under the internal revenue laws prior to reference to the Department of Justice. The Commissioner of Internal Revenue has the authority to compromise all taxes not in suit (Including any interest, penalty, additional amount or addition to tax) arising under the internal revenue laws except those relating to alcohol, tobacco, and firearms. This acceptance authority has been redelegated to certain Service officials depending on the jurisdiction of the case and the amount of the liability.

Basis For Compromise

The compromise of a tax liability can only rest on one or both of two grounds -
(1) doubt as to liability for the amount owed,
(2) doubt as to the collectibility of the full amount of tax, penalty and interest owed.

Section 7122 of the Internal Revenue Code does not confer authority to compromise tax, interest or penalty where the liability is determined by the courts and/or there is no doubt as to the ability of the Government to collect. In addition, the Service will not compromise, based on doubt as to liability, any penalty for failure to file information returns, failure to deposit taxes, or tendering bad checks. The doubt as to liability for the amount owed must be supported by evidence, and the amount acceptable will depend on the degree of doubt found in the particular case.

In the case of inability to pay, the amount offered must:
(1) exceed the total value of your equity in all your assets,
(2) give sufficient consideration to your present and future earning capacity, and
(3) you also must be in compliance with all paying and filing requirements for periods not included in the offer. This includes estimated payments, federal tax deposits, etc.

If your offer is acceptable we may require in addition to the above:
(1) a written collateral agreement to pay a percentage of future earnings as part of the offer,
(2) a written collateral agreement to relinquish certain present or potential tax benefits.

In the case of employment tax liabilities of an employer still in the same business as when the liability sought to be compromised was incurred, we will not accept your offer unless:
(1) it is equal to the unpaid tax liability, exclusive of penalties and interest,
(2) your financial condition is such that no greater amount can be collected,
(3) your current taxes are being paid by deposits as required.

Submission of an offer does not automatically suspend collection of an account. If there is any indication that the filing of the offer is solely for the purpose of delaying collection of the tax or that delay would negatively affect collection of the tax, we will continue collection efforts.

Interest and penalties will continue to accrue on the liability while your offer is under consideration. If your offer is accepted and all terms of the offer are satisfied (i.e., the offer and all collateral agreements are paid in full) we will abate the balance of the assessment. Please note: Interest will be due at the annual rate, as established under IRC section 6621(a), on any deferred portion of the offer from the date of notice of acceptance until it is paid in full.

Specific Instructions

1) Form 656, Offer in Compromise, must be used if you wish to submit an offer in compromise. The form should be prepared in duplicate and filed in any office of the Internal Revenue Service or directly to the Service Center servicing your area.

Form 433, Statement of Financial Condition and Other Information, must accompany Form 656 if the offer is based on doubt as to collectibility. Form 433 may be obtained at any IRS office. it is your responsibility to obtain Form 433 and fill it out completely so that we may adequately consider your offer.

2) Your full name, address, social security number and/or employer identification number should be entered on the top of Form 656. If this is a joint (husband and wife) liability and both wish to make an offer, one offer containing both names may be submitted. However, for any other joint liability, such as a partnership, separate offers must be submitted.

3) You should date the offer on the top of Form 656 in the space provided. This date is important for identification and reference purposes.

4) In item 1, you must list all unpaid tax liabilities sought to be compromised, regardless of type of tax. If you are singly liable (e.g. income taxes), separate tax entities exist and separate offers must be submitted. The type of tax and period involved must be specifically identified. Examples of the most common liabilities involved and the proper identification follows:

Wrong	.1040
Right	Income tax plus statutory additions for the year(s) 19xx...
Wrong	.941
Right	Withholding and Federal Insurance Contributions Act taxes plus statutory additions for the period(s) ended 9/30/xx, 12/31/xx...
Wrong	.940
Right	Federal Unemployment Tax Act taxes plus statutory additions for year(s) 19xx...
Wrong	.100% penalty
Right	100% penalty assessment plus statutory additions incurred as responsible person of Y Corporation for failure to pay withholding and Federal Insurance Contributions Act taxes for the periods ended 9/30/xx, 12/31/xx...
Wrong	Failure to file penalty
Right	Penalty for failure to file income tax return plus statutory addition for tax year(s) 19xx. (Note: This is necessary only if it is a separate offer submitted to compromise a penalty based on doubt as to liability.)

5) In Item 2, the total amount offered should be entered. If the offer is paid in full (i.e., the total amount is deposited with the offer) not other entry is required. If this is a deferred payment offer (i.e., any part of the offer is paid either on notice of acceptance or at any later date) you should show:

(a) the amount deposited at the time of filing this offer.

(b) any amount deposited on prior offers which are applied on this offer, and

(c) the amount of each deferred payment and the date on which each payment is to be made.

Example. $10,000 paid with the offer and balance of $25,000 to be paid at the rate of $5,000 per month beginning on the 15th day of the month following notice of acceptance and on the 15th day of each month thereafter.

The offer should be liquidated in the shortest time possible, and in no event will the payments extend more than six years. Interest is due at the prevailing Internal Revenue Code rate for any installment(s) due from the date of acceptance to the date of the full payment of the offer.

6) In Item 7, you must indicate the facts and reasons which are grounds for acceptance of the offer. If the offer is based on doubt as to collectibility, it is normally sufficient to state "I cannot pay these taxes." If your offer is based on doubt as to liability, then these grounds must be fully and completely explained. It would normally be necessary to attach a supporting statement.

7) Please sign the offer in the lower right hand corner of the form If you and your spouse seek to

compromise a joint income tax liability, both must sign. If the offer is to be signed by a person holding a power of attorney, the authorization must be direct and specific and authorize the representative to enter into a compromise of the specific liability.

8) You should be aware that on the Form 656, there are provisions for a waiver of refunds (item 3), a waiver of the statutory period of limitations for collection (item 6) and a waiver of the right to contest the liability after the offer is accepted (item 5). A delegated Service official will sign and date the appropriate block to accept the waiver of the statutory period of limitations for collection.

These instructions are intended only as an overview of the offer process and a guide in preparing Form 656. All forms necessary for filing an offer in compromise, plus additional information regarding the procedure can be obtained at local Internal Revenue Service offices.

There are several keys to compromising Federal tax liability. One key is to get fresh money from a third party non-obligor (spouse, parent, sibling, child, etc.) under no legal obligation to pay the tax.

A second key is to show the IRS that you have and will have nothing more to give them. The IRS may require you to sign a collateral agreement to pay them a percentage of significant increase in your earnings for a five year period. This protects the IRS if you win the lottery.

A third key is to convince the Offers In Compromise Section Chief that velocity of collection is more important to the IRS than having a lot of unpaid uncollectible tax liens on the books.

The fourth key is perseverance. Your request for compromise will probably be denied at the District Director level. You will have to appeal to the Appellate level. It appears that the Appellate level personnel have more discretionary powers to compromise and better judgment than the District level people. It may also be that the Appellate level decision maker has access to internal IRS production levels and objectives to be met.

The IRS may want to see your banking records and visit your home for a "life stye" inquiry prior to accepting the Offer in Compromise.

How To Deal With Lawsuits

You normally receive a summons and complaint when you are sued. Answer the summons or call the attorney or creditor issuing the summons.

Deal with them in the same manner as this manual indicates you should deal with credit managers. See How To Deal Directly With Your General Creditors in this manual.

Make a deal. Have the creditor agree to report to the Credit Reporting Agency that information about your account is not verifiable.

Most importantly, have the creditor's attorney file a Stipulation of Discontinuance of the action. This removes the lawsuit from your credit report. See the Form of Stipulation of Discontinuance.

How To Re-open Default Judgments

As discussed above, a lawsuit begins with a summons and complaint. If you don't answer the summons within a set number of days, a default Judgment will be taken against you.

A summons must be served personally upon you.

Most default Judgments occur because service other than personal service is used by the process servers. "Nail and Mail" and other forms of leaving a copy of the summons and complaint at your dwelling and mailing a second copy to you are considered valid substituted service, **provided that you actually learned of the lawsuit.**

If a default Judgment has been entered against you, go to the courthouse and read the affidavit of service attached by the process server to the summons. Most of the time the alleged service used will be nail and mail or other substituted service.

Sewer Service Is <u>Not</u> Good Service.

You can re-open a default Judgment for various reasons which vary from state to state. Usually the default is re-opened based upon a defect in the process service resulting in your never knowing about the case and your possessing a moritorious defense.

If the debt on which the Judgment was taken is valid and the creditor is a commercial operation, opening the default Judgment maybe obtained by agreeing to a workout or deferred payment plan if the creditor's attorney has not already attached your bank account or garnisheed your wages.

This agreement, usually called a Stipulation of Settlement, can include a provision to re-open the Judgment or at least stop execution of it while installment payments are made. Vacating by Order to Show Cause **will not** stop the continuation of the suit with its adverse credit effects. The Stipulation of Settlement should be used unless you have a defense sufficient to prevent losing the case. See Form Order To Show Cause To Re-Open A Default.

Speak with the clerk of the court in which a default judgment has been filed. The clerk will help you open the default and tell you what to do.

Judges are normally elected or appointed and are men of the people. **The court clerks learn from the judges. They are not your enemies.**

Priority Of Payment To Creditors

All creditors are not created equal. Certain creditors have greater legal rights than other creditors.

Don't waste your money by paying the wrong creditor, (unless you receive a hefty discount), until priority creditors are disposed of.

Tax liens are the most persistent and vexatious of liens to remove from your credit report. Normally, tax liens are not dischargeable in bankruptcy. There is no way to rid yourself of their liability. Furthermore, the interest and penalties can mount quickly. Your first priority should focus on paying tax liens by compromising the interest and penalties, if possible.

Moreover, tax liens are normally filed against both the husband and the wife, and can be satisfied from jointly held property. Other creditors have a claim against only one spouse.

You need the continued patronage of the life sustaining utilities like gas, electric, water and telephone companies. You cannot live without life-line utilities, so be sure to keep these creditors happy.

An effective way to deal with your other creditors is the ploy known as the "Tyranny of the Weak". After all, if you file personal bankruptcy, your credit report can't get worse and unsecured creditors get nothing. Sometimes your unsecured general creditors will be willing to settle their claims for new cash.

Inform your creditors that the source of the new funds is a relative, friend, or benefactor who has no obligation to pay your debts except to relieve your suffering in exchange for a substantial discount off what you owe.

How To Deal With Credit Reporting Agencies

As long as the Credit Reporting Agency does not think you are out to beat the system, (a) under advice from a credit repair clinic, or (b) by making "frivolous or irrelevant" claims, they are legally bound to listen to you and supplement their files with your side of the story.

If necessary, use Forms 615(b) and 606 in this book to obtain copies of your consumer investigative reports, if any; then use Forms 610 and 610 (b)-2 to arrange a visit to the Credit Reporting Agency and have them explain their file to you.

Then use Forms 611(a) and 611(b) in this book to update, amend, correct, delete and supplement the file with your version of the events.

Finally, use Form 611(d) and 611(d)-2 to force the Credit Reporting Agency to furnish notification of deletions of a disputed claim, or the filing of your consumer statement to any person who received the prior consumer report.

Remember, don't flood the Credit Reporting Agency with multiple requests to dispute your credit. You don't want to look like a credit repair clinic.

You get at least two (2) bites at the apple. If you can't resolve a dispute directly with the Credit Reporting Agency, you can always deal with your creditor.

Part V - Detailed Discussion Of The Finer Points Of The Fair Credit Reporting Act

A detailed discussion of the Fair Credit Reporting Act follows. We suggest that you will receive a better idea of how to deal with your Consumer Reporting Agency after understanding your rights.

Be advised that this analysis is based on the Fair Credit Reporting Act as in effect at the time of the printing of this book. It is possible for Congress to amend the Act in the future. No overhaul of the act was contemplated by Congress when this book was published.

Remember, the Consumer Reporting Agency is **not** your enemy. They only compile reports based upon what sources **including you** tell them about you.

The Fair Credit Reporting Act

(Public Law 91-508. Title 15, U.S.C. Sections 1601, et sec.)

GENERAL MATTERS:

The Federal Consumer Credit Reporting Act has as its short title: The Fair Credit Reporting Act, which serves as a 'nick-name'. The effective date of the Fair Credit Reporting Act was 1971.

THE LAW:

The entire statute is reproduced beginning on the following page for those who want to read the exact words of Congress.

CONSUMER CREDIT PROTECTION
SUBCHAPTER III - CREDIT REPORTING AGENCIES

1681. Congressional findings and statement of purpose

(a) The Congress makes the following findings:

(1) The banking system is dependent upon fair and accurate credit reporting. Inaccurate credit reports directly impair the efficiency of the banking system, and unfair credit reporting methods undermine the public confidence which is essential to the continued functioning of the banking system.

(2) An elaborate mechanism has been developed for investigating and evaluating the credit worthiness, credit standing, credit capacity, character, and general reputation of consumers.

(3) Consumer reporting agencies have assumed a vital role in assembling and evaluating consumer credit and other information on consumers.

(4) There is a need to insure that consumer reporting agencies exercise their grave responsibilities with fairness, impartiality, and a respect for the consumer's right to privacy.

(b) It is the purpose of this subchapter to require that consumer reporting agencies adopt reasonable procedures for meeting the needs of commerce for consumer credit, personnel, insurance, and other information in a manner which is fair and equitable to the consumer, with regard to the confidentiality, accuracy, relevancy, and proper utilization of such information in accordance with the requirements of this subchapter.

(Pub. L. 90-321, title VI, 602, as added Pub. L. 91-508, title VI, 601, Oct. 26, 1970, 84 Stat. 1128.)

EFFECTIVE DATE

Section 504(d) of Pub. L. 90-321, as added by Pub. L. 91-508. title VI, 602, Oct. 26, 1970, 84 Stat. 1136, provided that: "Title VI (enacting this subchapter) takes effect upon the expiration of one hundred and eighty days following the date of its enactment (Oct. 26, 1970)."

SHORT TITLE

This subchapter known as the "Fair Credit Reporting Act", see Short Title note set out under section 1601 of this title.

1681a. Definitions; rules of construction

(a) Definitions and rules of construction set forth in this section are applicable for the purposes of this subchapter.

(b) The term "person" means any individual, partnership, corporation, trust, estate, cooperative, association, government or governmental subdivision or agency, or other entity.

(c) The term "consumer" means an individual.

(d) The term "Consumer report" means any written, oral, or other communication of any information by a consumer reporting agency bearing on a consumer's credit worthiness, credit standing, credit capacity, character, general reputation, personal characteristics, or mode of living which is used or expected to be used or collected in whole or in part for the purpose of serving as a factor in establishing the consumer's eligibility for (1) credit or insurance to be used primarily for personal, family, or household purposes, or (2) employment purposes, or (3) other purposes authorized under section 1681b of this title. The term does not include (A) any report containing information solely as to transactions or experiences between the consumer and the person making the report; (B) any authorization or approval of a specific extension of credit directly or indirectly by the issuer of a credit card or similar device; or (C) any report in which a person who has been requested by a third party to make a specific extension of credit directly or indirectly to a consumer conveys his decision with respect to such request, if the third party advises the consumer of the name and address of the person to whom the request was made and such person makes the disclosures to the consumer required under section 1681m of this title.

(e) The term "investigative consumer report" means a consumer report or portion thereof in which information on a consumer's character, general reputation, personal characteristics, or mode of living is obtained through personal interviews with neighbors, friends, or associates of the consumer reported on or with others with whom he is acquainted or who may have knowledge concerning any such items of information. However, such information shall not include specific factual information on a consumer's credit record obtained directly from a creditor

of the consumer or from a consumer reporting agency when such information was obtained directly from a creditor of the consumer or from the consumer.

(f) The term "consumer reporting agency" means any person which, for monetary fees, dues, or on a cooperative nonprofit basis, regularly engages in whole or in part in the practice of assembling or evaluating consumer credit information or other information on consumers for the purpose of furnishing consumer reports to third parties, and which uses any means or facility of interstate commerce for the purpose of preparing or furnishing consumer reports.

(g) The term "file", when used in connection with information on any consumer, means all of the information on that consumer recorded and retained by a consumer reporting agency regardless of how the information is stored.

(h) The term "employment purposes" when used in connection with a consumer report means a report used for the purpose of evaluating a consumer for employment, promotion, reassignment or retention as an employee.

(i) The term "medical information" means information or records obtained, with the consent of the individual to whom it relates, from licensed physicians or medical practitioners, hospitals, clinics, or other medical or medically related facilities.

(Pub. L. 90-321, title VI. 603, as added Pub. L. 91-508, title VI, 601, Oct. 26, 1970, 84 Stat. 1128)

SECTION REFERRED TO IN OTHER SECTIONS

This section is referred to in sections 1692d, 1692e of this title; title 26 section 7609.

1681b. Permissible purposes of consumer reports

A consumer reporting agency may furnish a consumer report under the following circumstances and no other:

(1) In response to the order of a court having jurisdiction to issue such an order.

(2) In accordance with the written instructions of the consumer to whom it relates.

(3) To a person which it has reason to believe -

(A) intends to use the information in connection with a credit transaction involving the consumer on whom the information is to be furnished and involving the extension of credit to, or review or collection of an account of, the consumer; or

(B) intends to use the information for employment purposes; or

(C) intends to use the information in connection with the underwriting of insurance involving the consumer; or

(D) intends to use the information in connection with a determination of the consumer's eligibility for a license or other benefit granted by a government instrumentality required by law to consider an applicant's financial responsibility or status; or

(E) otherwise has a legitimate business need for the information in connection with a business transaction involving the consumer.

(Pub. L. 90-321, title VI, 604, as added Pub. L. 91-508, title VI, 601, Oct. 26, 1970, 84 Stat. 1129)

SECTION REFERRED TO IN OTHER SECTIONS

This section is referred to in sections 1681a, 1681e, 1681f, 1692d of this title.

1681c. Reporting of obsolete information prohibited

(a) Except as authorized under subsection (b) of this section, no consumer reporting agency may make any consumer report containing any of the following items of information:

(1) Cases under title 11 or under the Bankruptcy Act that, from the date of entry of the order for relief or the date of adjudication, as the case may be, antedate the report by more than 10 years.

(2) Suits and judgments which, from date of entry, antedate the report by more than seven years or until the governing statute of limitations has expired, whichever is the longer period.

(3) Paid tax liens which, from date of payment, antedate the report by more than seven years.

(4) Accounts placed for collection or charged to profit and loss which antedate the report by more than seven years.

(5) Records of arrest, indictment, or conviction of crime which, from date of disposition, release, or parole, antedate the report by more than seven years.

(6) Any other adverse item of information which antedates the report by more than seven years.

(b) The provisions of subsection (a) of this section are not applicable in the case of any consumer credit report to be used in connection with -

(1) a credit transaction involving, or which may reasonable be expected to involve, a principal amount of $50,000 or more;

(2) the underwriting of life insurance involving, or which may reasonably be expected to involve, a face amount of $50,000 or more; or

(3) the employment of any individual at an annual salary which equals, or which may reasonably be expected to equal $20,000, or more.

(Pub. L. 90-321, title VI, 605, as added Pub. L. 91-508, title VI, 601, Oct. 26, 1970, 84 Stat. 1129.)

(As amended Pub. L. 95-598, title III, 312(b), Nov. 6, 1978, 92 Stat. 2676.)

REFERENCES IN TEXT

Bankruptcy Act, referred to in subsec. (a)(1), was act July 1, 1898, ch. 541, 30 Stat. 544, as amended, which was classified to section 1 et seq. of former Title 11, Bankruptcy, prior to its repeal by Pub. L. 95-598, Nov. 6, 1978, 92 Stat. 2549, section 101 of which enacted revised Title 11.

AMENDMENTS

1978-Subsec. (a)(1). Pub. L. 95-598 substituted "cases under title 11 or under the Bankruptcy Act that, from the date of entry of the order for relief or the date of adjudication, as the case may be, antedate the report by more than 10 years" for "Bankruptcies which, from date of adjudication of the most recent bankruptcy, antedate the report by more than fourteen years".

EFFECTIVE DATE OF 1978 AMENDMENT

Amendment effective Oct. 1, 1979, see section 402(a) of Publ L. 95-598, set out as an Effective Date note preceding section 101 of Title 11, Bankruptcy.

SECTION REFERRED TO IN OTHER SECTIONS

This section is referred to in section 1681e of this title.

1681d. Disclosure of investigative consumer reports

(a) Disclosure of fact of preparation

A person may not procure or cause to be prepared an investigative consumer report on any consumer unless -

(1) it is clearly and accurately disclosed to the consumer that an investigative consumer report including information as to his character, general reputation, personal characteristics, and mode of living, whichever are applicable, may be made, and such disclosure (A) is made in a writing mailed, or otherwise delivered, to the consumer, not later than three days after the date on which the report was first requested, and (B) includes a statement informing the consumer of his right to request the additional disclosures provided for under subsection (b) of this section; or

(2) the report is to be used for employment purposes for which the consumer has not specifically applied.

(b) Disclosure on request of nature and scope of investigation

Any person who procures or causes to be prepared an investigative consumer report on any consumer shall, upon written request made by the consumer within a reasonable period of time after the receipt by him of the disclosure required by subsection (a)(1) of this section, shall make a complete and accurate disclosure of the nature and scope of the investigation requested. This disclosure shall be made in a writing mailed, or otherwise delivered, to the consumer not later than five days after the date on which the request for such disclosure was received from the consumer or such report was first requested, whichever is the later.

(c) Limitation on liability upon showing of reasonable procedures for compliance with provisions

No person may be held liable for any violation of subsection (a) or (b) of this section if he shows by a preponderance of the evidence that at the time of the violation he maintained reasonable procedures to assure compliance with subsection (a) or (b) of this section.

(Pub. L. 90-321, title VI, 606, as added Pub. l. 91-508, title VI, 601, Oct. 26, 1970, 84 Stat. 1130.)

1681e. Compliance procedures

(a) Every consumer reporting agency shall maintain reasonable procedures designed to avoid violations of section 1681c of this title and to limit the furnishing of consumer reports to the purposes listed under section 1681b of this title. These procedures shall require that prospective users of the information identify themselves, certify the purposes for which the information is sought, and certify that the information will be used for no other purpose. Every consumer reporting agency shall make a reasonable effort to verify the identity of a new prospective user and the uses certified by such prospective user prior to furnishing such user a consumer report. No consumer reporting agency may furnish a consumer report to any person if it has reasonable grounds for believing that the consumer report will not be used for a purpose listed in section 1681b of this title.

(b) Whenever a consumer reporting agency prepares a consumer report it shall follow reasonable procedures to assure maximum possible accuracy of the information concerning the individual about whom the report relates.

(Pub. L. 90-321, title VI, 607, as added Pub. L. 91-508, title VI, 601, Oct. 26, 1970, 84 Stat. 1130.) **1681f. Disclosures to governmental agencies**

Notwithstanding the provisions of section 1681b of this title, a consumer reporting agency may furnish identifying information respecting any consumer, limited to his name, address, former addresses, places of employment, or former places of employment, to a governmental agency.

(Pub. L. 90-321, title VI, 608, as added Pub. L. 91-508, title VI, 601, Oct. 26, 1970, 84 Stat. 1131.)

1681g. Disclosures to consumers

(a) Every consumer reporting agency shall, upon request and proper identification of any consumer, clearly and accurately disclose to the consumer:

(1) The nature and substance of all information (except medical information) in its files on the consumer at the time of the request.

(2) The sources of the information; except that the sources of information acquired solely for use in preparing an investigative consumer report and actually used for no other purpose need not be disclosed: Provided, That in the event an action is brought under this subchapter, such sources shall be available to the plaintiff under appropriate discovery procedures in the court in which the action is brought.

(3) The recipients of any consumer report on the consumer which it has furnished -

(A) for employment purposes within the two-year period preceding the request, and

(B) for any other purpose within the six-month period preceding the request.

(b) The requirements of subsection (a) of this section respecting the disclosure of sources of information and the recipients of consumer reports do not apply to information received or consumer reports furnished prior to the effective date of this subchapter except to the extent that the matter involved is contained in the file of the consumer reporting agency on that date.

(Pub. L. 90-321, title VI, 609, as added Pub. L. 91-508, title VI, 601, Oct. 26, 1970, 84 Stat. 1131.)

REFERENCES IN TEXT

For the effective date of this subchapter, referred to in subsec. (b), see section 504(d) of Pub. L. 90-321, set out as an Effective Date note under section 1681 of this title.

SECTION REFERRED TO IN OTHER SECTIONS

This section is referred to in sections 1681h, 1681j of this title.

1681h. Conditions of disclosure to consumers

(a) Times and notice

A consumer reporting agency shall make the disclosures required under section 1681g of this title during normal business hours and on reasonable notice.

(b) Identification of consumer

The disclosures required under section 1681g of this title shall be made to the consumer -

(1) in person if he appears in person and furnishes proper identification; or

(2) by telephone if he has made a written request, with proper identification, or telephone disclosure and the toll charge, if any, for the telephone call is prepaid by or charged directly to the consumer.

(c) Trained personnel

Any consumer reporting agency shall provide trained personnel to explain to the consumer any information furnished to him pursuant to section 1681g of this title.

(d) Persons accompanying consumer

The consumer shall be permitted to be accompanied by one other person of his choosing, who shall furnish reasonable identification. A consumer reporting agency may require the consumer to furnish a written statement granting permission to the consumer reporting agency to discuss the consumer's file in such person's presence.

(e) Limitation of liability

Except as provided in sections 1681n and 1681o of this title, no consumer may bring any action or proceeding in the nature of defamation, invasion of privacy, or negligence with respect to the reporting of information against any consumer reporting agency, any user of information, or any person who furnishes information to a consumer reporting agency, based on information disclosed pursuant to section 1681g, 1681h, or 1681m of this title, except as to false information furnished with malice or willful intent to injure such consumer.

(Pub. L. 90-321, title VI, 610, as added Pub. L. 91-508, title VI, 601, Oct. 26, 1970, 84 Stat. 1131.)

1681i. Procedure in case of disputed accuracy

(a) Dispute; reinvestigation

If the completeness or accuracy of any item of information contained in his file is disputed by a consumer, and such dispute is directly conveyed to the consumer reporting agency by the consumer, the consumer reporting agency shall within a reasonable period of time reinvestigate and record the current status of that information unless it has reasonable grounds to believe that the dispute by the consumer is frivolous or irrelevant. If after such reinvestigation such information is found to be inaccurate or can no longer be verified, the consumer reporting agency shall promptly delete such information. The presence of contradictory information in the consumer's file does not in and of itself constitute reasonable for believing the dispute is frivolous or irrelevant.

(b) Statement of dispute

If the reinvestigation does not resolve the dispute, the consumer may file a brief statement setting forth the nature of the dispute. The consumer reporting agency may limit such statement to not more than one hundred words if it provides the consumer with assistance in writing a clear summary of the dispute.

(c) Notification of consumer dispute in subsequent consumer reports

Whenever a statement of a dispute is filed, unless there is reasonable grounds to believe that it is frivolous or irrelevant, the consumer reporting agency shall, in any subsequent consumer report containing the information in question, clearly not that it is disputed by the consumer and provide either the consumer's statement or a clear and accurate codification or summary thereof.

(d) Notification of deletion of disputed information

Following any deletion of information which is found to be inaccurate or whose accuracy can no longer be verified or any notation as to disputed information, the consumer reporting agency shall, at the request of the consumer, furnish notification that the item has been deleted or the statement, codification or summary pursuant to subsection (b) or (c) of this section to any person specifically designated by the consumer who has within two years prior thereto received a consumer report for employment purposes, or within six months prior thereto received a consumer report for any other purpose, which contained the deleted or disputed information. The consumer reporting agency shall clearly and conspicuously disclose to the consumer his rights to make such a request. Such disclosure shall be made at or prior to the time the information is deleted or the consumer's statement regarding the disputed information is received.

(Pub. L. 90-321, title VI, 611, as added Pub. L. 91-508, title VI, 601, Oct. 26, 1970, 84 Stat. 1132.)

SECTION REFERRED TO IN OTHER SECTION

This section is referred to in section 1681j of this title.

1681j. Charges for disclosures

A consumer reporting agency shall make all disclosures pursuant to section 1681g of this title and furnish all consumer reports pursuant to section 1681i(d) of this title without charge to the consumer if, within thirty days after receipt by such consumer of a notification pursuant to section 1681m of this title or notification from a debt collection agency affiliated with such consumer reporting agency stating that the consumer's credit rating may be or has been adversely affected, the consumer makes a request under section 1681g or 1681j(d) of this title. Otherwise, the consumer reporting agency may impose a reasonable charge on the consumer for making disclosure to such consumer pursuant to section 1681g of this title, the charge for which shall be indicated to the consumer prior to making disclosure; and for furnishing notifications, statements, summaries, or codifications to person designated by the consumer pursuant to section 1681(d) of this title, the charge for which shall be indicated to the consumer prior to furnishing such information and shall not exceed the charge that the consumer reporting agency would impose on each designated recipient for a consumer report except that no charge may be made for notifying such persons of the deletion of information which is found to be inaccurate or which can no longer be verified.

(Pub. L. 90-321, title VI, 612, as added Pub. L. 91-508, title Vi, 601, Oct. 26, 1970, 84 Stat. 1132)

1681k. Public record information for employment purposes

A consumer reporting agency which furnishes a consumer report for employment purposes and which for that purpose compiles and reports items of information on consumers which are matters of public record and are likely to have an adverse effect upon a consumer's ability to obtain employment shall -

(1) at the time such public record information is reported to the user of such consumer report, notify the consumer of the fact that public record information is being reported by the consumer reporting agency, together with the name and address of the person to whom such information is being reported; or

(2) maintain strict procedures designed to insure that whenever public record information which is likely to have an adverse effect on a consumer's ability to obtain employment is reported it is complete and up to date. For purposes of this paragraph, items of public record relating to arrests, indictments, convictions, suits, tax lens, and outstanding judgments shall be considered up to date if the current public record status of the item at the time of the report is

reported.

(Pub. L. 90-321, title VI, 613, as added Pub. l. 91-508, title VI, 601, Oct. 26, 1970, 84 Stat. 1133.)

1681l. Restrictions on investigative consumer reports

Whenever a consumer reporting agency prepares an investigative consumer report, no adverse information in the consumer report (other than information which is a matter of public record) may be included in a subsequent consumer report unless such adverse information has been verified in the process of making such subsequent consumer report, or the adverse information was received with the three-month period preceding the date the subsequent report is furnished.

(Pub. L. 90-321, title VI, 614, as added Pub. L. 91-508, title VI, 601, Oct. 26, 1970, 84 Stat. 1133.)

1681m. Requirements on users of consumer reports

(a) Adverse action based on reports of consumer reporting agencies

Whenever credit or insurance for personal, family, or household purposes, or employment involving a consumer is denied or the charge for such credit or insurance is increased either wholly or partly because of information contained in a consumer report from a consumer reporting agency, the user of the consumer report shall so advise the consumer against whom such adverse action has been taken and supply the name and address of the consumer reporting agency making the report.

(b) Adverse action based on reports of persons other than consumer reporting agencies

Whenever credit for personal, family, or household purposes involving a consumer is denied or the charge for such credit is increased either wholly or partly because of information obtained from a person other than a consumer reporting agency bearing upon the consumer's credit worthiness, credit standing, credit capacity, character, general reputation, personal characteristics, or mode of living, the user of such information shall, within a reasonable period of time, upon the consumer's written request for the reasons for such adverse action received with sixty days after learning of such adverse action, disclose the nature of the information to the consumer. The user of such information shall clearly and accurately disclose to the consumer his right to make such written request at the time such adverse action is communicated to the consumer.

(c) Reasonable procedures to assure compliance

No person shall be held liable for any violation of this section if he shows by a preponderance of the evidence that at the time of the alleged violation he maintained reasonable procedures to assure compliance with the provisions of subsections (a) and (b) of this section.

(Pub. L. 90-321, title VI, 615, as added Pub. L. 91-508, title VI, 601, Oct. 26, 1970, 84 Stat. 1133.)

SECTION REFERRED TO IN OTHER SECTIONS

This section is referred to in sections 1681a, 1681h, 1681j of this title.

1681n. Civil liability for willful noncompliance

Any consumer reporting agency or user of information which willfully fails to comply with any requirement imposed under this subchapter with respect to any consumer is liable to that consumer in an amount equal to the sum of -

(1) any actual damages sustained by the consumer as a result of the failure;

(2) such amount of punitive damages as the court may allow; and

(3) in the case of any successful action to enforce any liability under this section, the costs of the action together with reasonable attorney's fees as determined by the court.

(Pub. L. 90-321, title VI, 616, as added Pub. L. 91-508, title VI, 601, Oct. 26, 1970, 84 Stat. 1134.)

SECTION REFERRED TO IN OTHER SECTIONS

This section is referred to in section 1681h of this title.

1681o. Civil liability for negligent noncompliance

Any consumer reporting agency or user of information which is negligent in failing to comply with any requirement imposed under this subchapter with respect to any consumer is liable to that consumer in an amount equal to the sum of -

(1) any actual damages sustained by the consumer as a result of the failure;

(2) in the case of any successful action to enforce any liability under this section, the costs of the action together with reasonable attorney's fees as determined by the court.

(Pub. L. 90-321, title VI, 617, as added Pub. L. 91-508, title VI, 601, Oct. 26, 1970, 84 Stat. 1134.)

SECTION REFERRED TO IN OTHER SECTIONS

This section is referred to in section 1681h of this title.

681p. Jurisdiction of courts; limitation of actions

An action to enforce any liability created under this subchapter may be brought in any appropriate United States district court without regard to the amount in controversy, or in any other court of competent jurisdiction, within two years from the date on which the liability arises, except that where a defendant has materially and willfully misrepresented any information required under this subchapter to be disclosed to an individual and the information so misrepresented is material to the establishment of the defendant's liability to that individual under this subchapter, the action may be brought at any time within two years after discovery by the individual of the misrepresentation.

(Pub. L. 90-321, title VI, 618, as added Pub. L. 91-508, title VI, 601, Oct. 26, 1970, 84 Stat. 1134.)

681q. Obtaining information under false pretenses

Any person who knowingly and willfully obtains information on a consumer from a consumer reporting agency under false pretenses shall be fined not more than $5,000 or imprisoned not more than one year, or both.

(Pub. L. 90-321, title VI, 619, as added Pub. L. 91-508, title VI, 601, Oct. 26, 1970, 84 Stat. 1134.)

1681r. Unauthorized disclosures by officers or employees

Any officer or employee of a consumer reporting agency who knowingly and willfully provides information concerning an individual from the agency's files to a person not authorized to receive that information shall be fined not more than $5,000 or imprisoned not more than one year, or both.

(Pub. L. 90-321, title VI, 620, as added Pub. L. 91-508, title VI, 601, Oct. 26, 1970, 84 Stat. 1134.)

1681s. Administrative enforcement

(a) Federal Trade Commission; powers

Compliance with the requirements imposed under this subchapter shall be enforced under the Federal Trade Commission Act (15 U.S.C. 41 et seq.) by the Federal Trade Commission with respect to consumer reporting agencies and all other persons subject thereto, except to the extent that enforcement of the requirements imposed under this subchapter is specifically committed to some other government agency under subsection (b) hereof. For the purpose of the exercise by the Federal Trade Commission of its functions and powers under the Federal Trade Commission Act, a violation of any requirement or prohibition imposed under this subchapter shall constitute an unfair or deceptive act or practice in commerce in violation of section 5(a) of the Federal Trade Commission Act (15 U.S.C. 45(a)) and shall be subject to enforcement by the Federal Trade Commission under section 5(b) thereof (15 U.s.C. 45(b)) with respect to any consumer reporting agency or person subject to enforcement by the Federal Trade Commission pursuant to this subsection, irrespective of whether that person is engaged in commerce or meets any other jurisdictional tests in the Federal Trade Commission Act. The Federal Trade Commission shall have such procedural rules in enforcing compliance with the requirements imposed under this subchapter and to require the filing of reports, the production of documents, and the appearance of witnesses as though the applicable terms and condition of the Federal Trade Commission Act were part of this subchapter. Any person violating any of the provisions of this subchapter shall be subject to the penalties and entitled to the privileges and immunities provided in the Federal Trade Commission Act as though the applicable terms and provisions thereof were part of this subchapter.

(b) Other administrative bodies

Compliance with the requirements imposed under this subchapter with respect to consumer reporting agencies and persons who use consumer reports from such agencies shall be enforced under -

(1) section 8 of the Federal Deposit Insurance Act (12 U.S.C. 1818), in the case of:

(A) national banks, by the Comptroller of the Currency;

(B) member banks of the Federal Reserve System (Other than national banks), by the Federal Reserve Board; and

(C) banks insured by the Federal Deposit Insurance Corporation (other than members of the Federal Reserve System), by the Board of Directors of the Federal Deposit Insurance Corporation.

(2) section 5(d) of the Home Owners Loan Act of 1933 (12 U.S.C. 1464(d)), section 407 of the National Housing Act (12 U.S.C. 1730), and sections 6(i) and 17 of the Federal Home Loan Bank Act (12 U.S.C. 1426(i) and 1437), by the Federal Home Loan Bank Board (acting directly or through the Federal Savings and Loan Insurance Corporation), in the case of any institution subject to any of those provisions;

(3) the Federal Credit Union Act (12 U.S.C. 1751 et

seq.), by the Administrator of the National Credit Union Administrator of the National Credit Union Administration with respect to any Federal credit union;

(4) the Acts to regulate commerce, by the Interstate Commerce Commission with respect to any common carrier subject to those Acts;

(5) the Federal Aviation Act of 1958 (49 U.S.C. 1301 et seq.), by the Civil Aeronautics Board with respect to any air carrier or foreign air carrier subject to that Act; and

(6) the Packers and Stockyards Act, 1921 (7 U.S.C. 181 et seq.) (except as provided in section 406 of that Act (7 U.S.C. 226, 227)), by the Secretary of Agriculture with respect to any activities subject to that Act.

(c) Enforcement under other authority

For the purpose of the exercise by any agency referred to in subsection (b) of this section of its powers under any Act referred to in that subsection, a violation of any requirement imposed under this subchapter shall be deemed to be a violation of a requirement imposed under that Act. In addition to its powers under any provision of law specifically referred to in subsection (b) of this section, each of the agencies referred to in that subsection may exercise, for the purpose of enforcing compliance with any requirement imposed under this subchapter any other authority conferred on it by law.

(Pub. L. 90-321, title VI, 621, as added Pub. L. 91-508, title VI, 601, Oct. 26, 1970, 84 Stat. 1134.)

CODIFICATION

The Acts to regulate commerce, referred to in subsec. (b)(4), are known as the Interstate Commerce Act (act Feb. 4, 1887, ch. 104, 24 Stat. 379, as amended), which was classified to chapters 1 (1 et seq.), 8 (301 et seq.), 12 (901 et seq.), 13 (1001 et seq.), and 19 (12331 et seq.) of Title 49, Transportation. The Act was repealed by Pub. L. 95-473, 4(b), Oct. 17, 1978, 92 Stat. 1467, the first section of which enacted subtitle IV (10101 et seq.) of Title 49. For distribution of former sections of Title 49 into the revised Title 49, see Table at the beginning of Title 49.

TERMINATION OF CIVIL AERONAUTICS BOARD AND TRANSFER OF CERTAIN FUNCTIONS

All functions, powers, and duties of the Civil Aeronautics Board were terminated or transferred by section 1551 of Title 49, Transportation, effective in part on Dec. 31 1981, in part on Jan 1, 1983, and in part on Jan. 1, 1985.

REFERENCES IN TEXT

The Federal Trade Commission Act, referred to in subsec. (a), is act Sept. 26, 1914, ch. 311, 38 Stat. 717, which is classified generally to subchapter I (41 et seq.) of chapter 2 of this title. For complete classification of this Act to the Code, see section 58 of this title and Tables volume.

The Federal Credit Union Act, referred to in subsec. (b)(3), is act June 26, 1934, ch. 750, 48 Stat. 1216, which is classified generally to chapter 14 (1751 et seq.) of Title 12, Banks and Banking. For complete classification of this Act to the Code, see section 1751 of Title 12 and Tables volume.

The Acts to regulate commerce, referred to in subsec. (b)(4), are known as the Interstate Commerce Act (act Feb. 4, 1887, ch. 104, 24 Stat. 379, as amended), which is classified generally to chapters 1 (1 et seq.), 8 (301 et seq.), 12 (901 et seq.), 13 (1001 et seq.), and 19 (1231 et seq.) of Title 49, Transportation. For complete classification of this Act to the Code, see note captioned Interstate Commerce Act set out under section 27 of Title 49 and Tables volume.

The Federal Aviation Act of 1958, referred to in subsec. (b)(5), is Pub. L. 85-726, Aug. 23, 1958, 72 Stat. 737, which is classified generally to chapter 20 (1301 et seq.) of Title 49, Transportation. For complete classification of this Act to the Code, see Short Title note set out under section 1301 of Title 49 and Tables volume.

1681t. Relation to State laws

This subchapter does not annul, alter, affect, or exempt any person subject to the provisions of this subchapter from complying with the laws of any State with respect to the collection, distribution, or use of any information on consumers, except to the extent that those laws are inconsistent with any provision of this subchapter, and then only to the extent of the inconsistency.

(Pub. L. 90-321, title VI, 622, as added Pub. L. 91-508, title VI, 601, Oct. 26, 1970, 84 Stat. 1136.)

Detailed Discussion Of The Act

Findings Of Congress

Congress made certain findings and a statement of purposes underlying the need for the Fair Credit Reporting Act.

1 - The banking system is dependent upon **fair** and **accurate** credit reporting.

2 - Inaccurate credit reports impair the efficiency of the banking system.

3 - Unfair credit methods undermine public confidence which is essential to the banking system.

4 - Consumer Reporting Agencies have assumed a vital role in assembling and evaluating the credit worthiness, credit standing, credit capacity, character and general reputation of consumers.

5 - A **need** exists to insure that Consumer Reporting Agencies exercise their **grave responsibility** with fairness, impartiality, and a **respect** for the consumer's right to privacy.

Congress' Purposes

Congress stated its purposes in passing the Fair Credit Reporting Act **to protect you** as follows:

"It is the purpose of this [law] to require that Consumer Reporting Agencies adopt reasonable procedures for meeting the needs of commerce for consumer credit, personnel, insurance, and other information in a manner which is **fair and equitable to the consumer** with regard to the **confidentiality, accuracy, relevancy, and proper utilization of such information** in accordance with this [law]. (emphasis added)

Importance Of Congress' Findings And Statement Of Purpose

Congress legitimatized the Consumer Reporting Agencies - to exercise their grave responsibility
- with fairness
- impartiality
- and a respect for your right to privacy by adopting reasonable procedures for assimilating information in a manner fair and equitable to you
- with respect to confidentiality, accuracy, and relevancy.

You Are A Consumer !

'Consumer' means an individual under the Fair Credit Reporting Act, as compared to a group, partnership, company or union which are not deemed to be consumers.

Consumer Reports

Credit Reporting Agencies assemble, prepare and distribute Consumer Reports.

A Consumer Report is any written or oral or other communication of information by a consumer reporting agency bearing on your
- credit worthiness
- credit standing
- credit capacity
- character
- general reputation
- personal characteristics
- or mode of living

used, collected or a factor in establishing your eligibility for
- credit or insurance
  (primarily for personal, family or household purposes, employment purposes) or employment, promotion, reassignment, or retention as an employee.

Consumer reports can also be used in certain transactions (a) involving extensions of credit, (b) in connection with underwriting insurance, (c) involving license or other benefits granted by a governmental instrumentality, (d) to consider an applicant's financial responsibility or status, (e) or, in connection with a legitimate business need for information involving you (i.e. an investment lease agreement, franchise or partnership or other legitimate business transaction). Consumer reports can also be furnished in response to a court order, or in accordance with your written instructions.

Who Can Get A Copy Of Your Consumer Credit Report?

Under the Fair Credit Reporting Act, the availability of access to your credit file is strictly controlled, with a severe criminal penalties of a $5,000 fine and one year's imprisonment for unauthorized disclosures.

Only the following persons are allowed access to your credit file:

1 - Those authorized in writing by you.
2 - Creditors to whom you have applied for credit.
3 - Insurers whom you have asked for coverage.
4 - Employers.
5 - Potential employers.
6 - Those who have a definite business purpose related to a business transaction involving you (a lease, for example).
7 - Governmental agencies.
8 - By order of a Court of competent jurisdiction.

Whenever a person orders a copy of your consumer credit report, the inquiry is noted in your credit file.

You are entitled to know the identity of any person who has requested your credit file within the past six (6) months or two (2) years, if the inquiry was for employment purposes.

This recipient identity report is provided when you order a copy of your credit report, and is necessary so that if, as and when you improve your credit listing, you can have copies of the improved credit report furnished to prior recipients of the old report.

Furthermore, Consumer Reporting Agencies must establish security procedures to prevent anyone without a legitimate business purpose from obtaining your credit report. In fact, Section 620 of the Fair Credit Reporting Act makes it a crime for any officer or employee of a Consumer Reporting Agency to knowingly and willfully provide information to an unauthorized person.

Moreover, Section 619 of the Fair Credit Reporting Act makes it a crime (punishable by a $5,000 fine and one (1) year's imprisonment), for any unauthorized person to obtain consumer credit information under false pretenses.

Even with the severe bite of the criminal law and the best security in place, breaches of security and unauthorized access to credit files do sometimes occur. **Accordingly, it is important to verify who has had access to your credit file.**

Examples Of What Are And Are Not Consumer Reports

A report used to establish a customer's eligibility for business, trade or occupationally associated credit is not a consumer report.

If the credit or insurance is not **primarily** to be for personal, family or household purposes, then the report is NOT a consumer report.

Primarily means the Fair Credit Reporting Act does not apply to credit reports on:
- occupational matters
- farmers
- agricultural
- doctors
- sole partnerships

Certain esoteric exceptions exist applying to; additional in-house credit extensions on existing credit lines, and; communications between a creditor and credit reporting agency involving the creditor's own ledger experience. Each of these are NOT deemed consumer reports.

Who Is A Consumer Reporting Agency?

A Consumer Reporting Agency is any person, who, for monetary fees, dues or on a cooperative non-profit basis regularly engages in whole or in part in assembling or evaluating consumer credit information, or other information on consumers for furnishing consumer reports to third parties and uses any means or facility of interstate commerce for the purpose of preparing or furnishing consumer reports.

Compliance Procedures Of Credit Reporting Agencies

Consumer Reporting Agencies **must** maintain **reasonable procedures** to **update obsolete information** and **only furnish consumer reports to authorized users for legitimate purposes.**

Section 607 of the Fair Credit Reporting Act is the key section which establishes potential liability on the part of the Consumer Reporting Agency for failure to establish and maintain reasonable procedures to avoid making mistakes concerning obsolete information, inaccurate information, and improper dissemination of consumer reports.

Thus, Consumer Reporting Agencies have the liability and responsibility to you, for operating an agency in a responsible manner and disseminating current, accurate information only to authorized users.

Furthermore, every Consumer Reporting Agency **must follow reasonable procedures to insure maximum possible accuracy** of the information concerning the individual about whom the report relates.

Civil litigation against Consumer Reporting Agencies is normally brought under this section.

Agency's Duty To Update Obsolete Information

Every Consumer Reporting Agency must maintain reasonable procedures to avoid including obsolete information in their consumer reports. (Section 607 of the Fair Credit Reporting Act.)

What Constitutes Obsolete Information

The following is considered obsolete information which must be purged by a Credit Reporting Agency from its credit report.

1 - Bankruptcy cases more than ten (10) years old. However, most Credit Reporting Agencies drop Chapter 13 cases (Adjustment of Debts of an individual with regular income) after seven (7) years.

2 - Suits and Judgments more than seven (7) years old or until the statute of limitations has expired, whichever is longer. (Civil Judgments normally have a ten (10) year life and if renewed, may be extended for a further period.) Most Credit Reporting Agencies under the regulations promulgated by the Associated Credit Bureaus, Inc., report lawsuits for a two (2) year limit unless disposition has been determined or unless the case is known to be still pending before the court.

3 - Paid tax liens more than seven (7) years old.

4 - Although the law specifies no time for reporting unpaid tax liens, the Associated Credit Bureau, Inc., recommends that credit reporting agencies re-check public records before reporting tax liens unpaid after seven (7) years.

5 - Accounts placed for collection or charged-off accounts which are seven (7) years old. The Federal Trade Commission's view is that the seven (7) year period begins from the last charge or payment prior to the charge-off. Accordingly, subsequent payments or automatic accruals of interest do not start the seven (7) year period over again.

6 - Records of arrest, indictment or convictions of a crime more than seven (7) years old. If the criminal case was dismissed or the consumer found not guilty, the indictment or the case should no longer be reported in a consumer report.

7 - Any other adverse item of information more than seven (7) years old.

8 - There is no time limitation whatsoever for reporting favorable or neutral data.

9 - The duty to delete unfavorable or derogatory information after seven (7) years does not apply to credit transactions involving a principal amount of $50,000 or more, or employment information for a job at an annual salary which equals or exceeds $20,000.

OBSOLETE & ADVERSE INFORMATION CHART

Item of Information	Number of Years on Your Credit Report	Comments
Bankruptcy	10 years	
Judgments	7 years or State Statute of Limitations on Judgments, whichever is longer	Longer of 7 years under Federal Law or Statute of Limitations under State Law which could be 10 years plus a renewal period of 10 years
Chapter 13	7 years	
Paid Tax Lien	7 years	
Unpaid Tax Lien	Indefinite	Subject to reverification by credit bureaus after 7 years
Accounts placed for Collection	7 years	From charge-off
Charged-Off Accounts	7 years	From last charge statement or last payment prior to charge-off according to Federal Trade Commission interpretation
Conviction of Crime	7 years	From disposition, parole or release
Any other adverse information	7 years	
Lawsuits against you	2 years	Unless disposition has been sooner determined or case is still known to be pending
Records of Arrest or Indictment	Should be deleted immediately if you are found not guilty or if case is dropped	

Disclosures To You Of Your Files By A Consumer Reporting Agency

Section 609 of the Fair Credit Reporting Act compels every Consumer Reporting Agency, upon your request and proper identification, to clearly and accurately disclose to you:
- the nature and substance of all information (except medical information) in its files at the time of the request, and
- the sources of the information
- the recipients of any consumer report on you for employment purposes within the last two (2) years and for any other purpose within the six (6) months preceding the request.

Except that the following need not be disclosed:
- The sources of information acquired solely for use in preparing an investigative consumer report and actually used for another purpose. See the discussion concerning Investigative Consumer Reports in this Manual.
- Sources of information received and recipients of consumer reports furnished prior to the 1971 effective date of the Fair Credit Reporting Act.

The term 'file' means all of the information on you recorded and retained by a Consumer Reporting Agency regardless of how the information is stored.

The term 'employment purposes' means a report used for the purpose of evaluating a consumer for employment, promotion, reassignment or retention as an employee.

The term 'medical information' means information or records obtained, with the consent of the individual to whom it relates, from licensed physicians or medical practitioners, hospitals, clinics, or other medically related facilities.

Accordingly, under Section 609, the Credit Reporting Agency is under a duty to disclose the nature and substance of all information to you no matter how the information is filed, coded or maintained.

While the Credit Reporting Agency need not disclose medical information contained in your health record as reported by a doctor or hospital to an insurance company, it is required to disclose credit information concerning payments to doctors and hospitals. You can ask your doctor about your medical health.

Notification To Consumer Of Adverse Action By User Of A Consumer Report

Section 615 is the trigger for all of your rights under the Fair Credit Reporting Act. Whenever you are denied credit, insurance or employment, or the rate for the credit is increased either wholly or in part because of information in a consumer report, the user of the information **must advise** you of the **adverse decision** and **must** supply the name and address of the Credit Reporting Agency making the report. **This gives rise to your ability to refute, update and dispute inaccurate or obsolete information and to otherwise tell your side of the story.**

NOTE: This applies only to consumer credit for personal, family or household purposes and reviews an earlier discussion that the Fair Credit Reporting Act does not cover business, professional or agricultural debt.

The creditor-user may notify you orally or in writing. We believe most users respond in writing with a pre-printed form.

Conditions And Charges A Consumer Reporting Agency May Set Prior To Its Duty To Disclosure To You Of Your File

Section 610 of the Fair Credit Reporting Act sets certain universal conditions you must meet before a Consumer Reporting Agency discloses its file to you and Section 612 establishes the charges.

A Consumer Reporting Agency must disclose its files on you to you:

A - ON YOUR PERSONAL APPEARANCE
- By trained personnel with experience and knowledge of your file and the law, during its normal business hours, upon reasonable notice by you at your request and furnishing of proper identification, or if you are accompanied by one other person of your choosing who shall furnish reasonable identification.

B - BY TELEPHONE
- If you have made a prior written request (See Form 610(b)(2) for telephone disclosure and paid or pre-paid the telephone toll charge, if any.

The Fair Debt Reporting Act does not describe exact procedures for proper identification. The test is reasonableness. A drivers license, credit card or knowledge of your prior credit listing and social security number, date of birth, etc. should suffice.

a) Personal Appearance - Common sense and good business practice would indicate that an appointment for a personal visit would be helpful for both you and the Credit Reporting Agency. An appointment would minimize everyone's time and your anxiety.

You may bring another person of your choosing with you in addition to your spouse during the interview at the agency. This person may be an interpreter, friend, neighbor, attorney, or someone whose common sense and judgment you respect. This other person must provide reasonable identification. You may have to sign a statement granting the credit reporting agency permission to discuss your file in this person's presence. See Form 610 - Request For Personal Interview With Consumer Reporting Agency.

b) Telephone Interview - Section 610(b)(2) provides for a telephone interview upon **prior written request by you** for the complete disclosure.

Form 610(b)(2) deals with your written request for a telephone interview for disclosure of all information on you in the agency's files.

Credit Reporting Agencies may have their own request for telephone interview form, and will call you back collect because you must pay the telephone charges. See Form 610(b)(2) Request For Telephone Interview With Consumer Reporting Agency.

Charges

The Credit Reporting Agency may **not** charge you for disclosure to you of your file, if within the prior thirty (30) days you received:
- a debt collection notice from an affiliate of that credit reporting agency, or
- notice of an adverse credit determination denying you credit or increasing charges wholly or partly as a result of a credit report from such agency.

Otherwise, the Credit Reporting Agency **may impose a reasonable charge** which must be indicated to you for making disclosure and for furnishing notifications, statement summaries, or codifications at your request to persons you designate under the procedures in case of disputed accuracy under Section 611(d) of the Act.

In no event shall the charge to you **exceed** the charge the Consumer Reporting Agency imposes on its own customers who are users and recipients of the credit report for the same information.

Furthermore, under no circumstances can the Consumer Reporting Agency charge you for notifying a prior recipient of the report of the deletion of information found to be inaccurate or which can no longer be verified.

The Consumer Reporting Agency **may** charge you a fee to contact new references or verify new data to be added to your file as opposed to verifying new balances or collecting information in the file.

CREDIT REPORTING AGENCY FEE CHART

	* Within 30 Days of Notification of Adverse Credit Determination or Collection Letter.	* After 30 Days Notification of Adverse Determination or Collection Letter.
Your Request	No Fee	Reasonable Fee
Personal Appearance Form 610	No Fee	Reasonable fee not to exceed the charges to its own creditor-users
Telephone Request to Obtain a Copy of Your Consumer Report Form 610(b)(2)	No Fee	Reasonable fee plus collect telephone charge
Notice of Disputed Accuracy Form 611(a)	No Fee	No Fee
Deletion of Inaccrate or Unverifiable Information Form 611a	No Fee	No Fee
Verifying New Data to be Added to Your File Form Supplemental-1	Reasonable Fee	Reasonable Fee
Furnishing Notification of Deletion of Disputed Items to Persons Who Received the Prior Consumer Report Forms 611(d) & 611(d)(2)	No Fee	Reasonable Fee
Filing a Consumer Statement Form 611(b)	No Fee	No Fee
Deletion of Obsolete Information Form 607	No Fee	Reasonable Fee
Furnishing Notification of Consumer Statement to Persons Who Received the Prior Consumer Report Forms 611(d) & 611(d)(2)	No Fee	Reasonable Fee
Reasons for Adverse Action - User of Credit Information Received from 3rd Party Form 615(b)	Within 60 Days of Notification of Adverse Action (No Fee)	After 60 Days of Notification of Action (No Fee provided for in Statute. Statute is silent.)
Ordering a Copy of an Investigative Consumer Report Form 606	Within a reasonable time No Fee	After a reasonable time (Statute is silent)
For Women to Open a Credit File in Their Own Name Form EOCC-1	No Fee	No Fee

MOST CREDIT REPORTING AGENCIES WILL EXTEND THIS THIRTY DAY PERIOD TO SIXTY DAYS BECAUSE THEY ARE NOT CERTAIN OF EXACTLY WHEN YOU ACTUALLY RECEIVED THE NOTICES.

Procedure In The Case Of Disputed Accuracy (Section 611 Of The Act)

If you dispute the completeness or accuracy of any item of information in your file and directly convey your dispute to the Consumer Reporting Agency (See Form 611a), the agency has a reasonable amount of time to reinvestigate and record the current status of that information unless it has reasonable grounds to believe your dispute is frivolous or irrelevant.

After reinvestigation, if disputed information is found to be inaccurate or can no longer be verified, the Consumer Reporting Agency must promptly delete the disputed information from your consumer report. This situation often arises when a store or finance company or utility has no current record of a previously charged-off account. Most data banks can only access a limited amount of data and many businesses prioritize current information and wipe-out old information on uncollected accounts.

Furthermore, the Fair Credit Reporting Act states that the presence of contradictory information in your file provided by the user-credit grantor-customer of the agency does not in and of itself contribute reasonable grounds for believing your dispute is frivolous or irrelevant.

Your Credit Reporting Agency must delete disputed items or inaccurate information that cannot be reverified after reinvestigation. They will maintain the integrity of the credit file and will process your requests for verification with the same courtesy and promptness they afford their own customers who are credit users. See Form 611(a) Notice Of Disputed Claim To The Credit Reporting Agency.

Your Right To Make A Statement If Reinvestigation Does Not Resolve The Dispute (Section 611(b) of the Act)

If reinvestigation does not resolve the dispute, you may file a brief statement setting forth the nature of the dispute. See Form 611(b) for a form of consumer statement.

After you have filed your consumer statement, the Consumer Reporting Agency **must** tell your side of the story in any future consumer reports containing the information in question, unless it has reasonable grounds to believe the dispute is frivolous or irrelevant. The agency may either provide a copy of your consumer statement or a clear and accurate codification or summary of your consumer statement.

A clear and accurate codification of your consumer statement occurs in a computerized credit reports where the computer may have a code which represents the fact that you did not order, authorize a purchase, or returned a disputed item to the seller.

The Consumer Reporting Agency may limit your consumer statement to not more then one hundred (100) words if it provides you with assistance in writing a clear summary of the dispute. See Form 611(d) Consumer Statement.

Your Rights To Notify The World That A Disputed Item Is Deleted Information Or That You Filed A Consumer Statement 611(d) of the Fair Credit Reporting Act

After investigation, the disputed item is either deleted or you file a consumer statement disputing the item and telling your side of the story. See Form 611(d).

You have the additional right to request that the Consumer Reporting Agency inform everyone of the deletion or of your consumer statement, if the person received the consumer report within the past two (2) years for employment purposes or for any other purpose within the past six (6) months.

There should be no charge for this renotification of deletion or consumer statement if the request is made by you within thirty (30) days after (a) receipt of an adverse credit determination about you, or (b) a notification from a debt collection agency affiliated with the consumer reporting agency trying to collect from you.

After such thirty day period, the Fair Credit Reporting Act provides that the Consumer Reporting Agency may make a reasonable charge for notifications, and statements forwarded to previous recipients at your request as long as the charge is stated to you in advance and does not exceed the amount charged by the agency to its own user-customers for the same information.

See Form 611(d) for a form of request to furnish notification of deletion of disputed item or filing of a consumer statement within thirty days after receipt of adverse credit decision or collection letter.

See Form 611(d)-2 for a form of request to furnish notification of deletion of a disputed item or filing of a consumer statement more than thirty days following receipt of adverse credit decision or collection letter and tendering of fees.

Investigative Consumer Reports

Investigative Consumer Reports contain information on a your character, general reputation, personal characteristics or mode of living obtained from **personal interviews** with neighbors, friends, associates, or others with whom you are acquainted. Investigative Consumer Reports contain information about your friends, personal habits, morals or lifestyle.

Seldom, if ever, do consumer reporting agencies develop Investigative Consumer Reports. They are generally prepared for insurance companies or for employment-personnel matters and are normally prepared by specialized companies other than credit bureaus.

But lifestyle information could conceivably find its way into or be appended to your consumer report or find its way to creditor-users. This is why this section is in the manual. Protect your rights.

With one exception relating to unapplied for employment, **no one** can procure an investigative consumer report about you without your knowledge, consent and ability to respond to derogatory, unfavorable information or snide inferences contained in that report.

Under Section 606 of the Fair Credit Reporting Act, a person (any individual, partnership, organization, trust, estate, cooperative, association, government or governmental subdivision or agency or other entity is defined as a person under the Act), may not procure or prepare an investigative consumer report about you without a clear and accurate disclosure to you, in writing, mailed or delivered to you not later than three (3) days after the consumer investigative report was first requested. Also, a statement informing you of **your right** to request additional disclosures under the Fair Credit Reporting Act, to learn the complete nature and scope of the investigation.

The **user** of the consumer investigative report must respond to your written request for a complete and accurate disclosure of the nature and scope of the investigation on you in writing, mailed or delivered to you not later than five (5) days after the written request for such additional disclosure was first received from the consumer or the investigative consumer report was requested, whichever is later.

You must make the written request within a **reasonable time** after you receive the written notice that an investigative consumer report may be requested.

Beware ! The written notice from the User (usually an insurance company, bank or employer) **may be included on an application or handed to you - but it must be in writing** !

The only exception to the written notice to you that a person has requested an investigative consumer report concerning you occurs if the report is used for employment purposes for which you **have not** specifically applied.

This exception allows an employer to screen an individual whom the employer **might** recruit for a position or promote or transfer **without** notifying that consumer that an investigative consumer report is being compiled. Congress recognized that an employer may wish to examine the qualifications of several people before offering any one of them a job, promotion or transfer. Congress deemed advance notification of the employment search on **non-specifically applied for** employment situations less important than the employer's right to search for qualified candidates.

However, if you have applied for a job and a consumer investigative report is ordered, the prospective employer must notify you within three (3) days after ordering the report, of your right to make a written request to receive accurate disclosure of the nature and scope of the investigation. See Form 606 Request For A Copy Of An Investigative Consumer Report.

Restrictions On Re-use Of Investigative Consumer Reports

No adverse information in an investigative consumer report (other than public records) can be reissued in another investigative consumer report unless the adverse information has been verified again in the process of making the second report or unless the adverse information is not more than three (3) months old.

Section 614 of the Fair Credit Reporting Act recognizes that Consumer Reporting Agencies recycle adverse information and places a high standard on them to **reverify adverse hearsay information or opinions** made by employers about employees, neighbors about neighbors, and friends about friends. Current information (less than three (3) months old) need not be updated or reverified.

Notification To Consumer Of Adverse Action Because Of Information Obtained From A Person Other Than A Consumer Reporting Agency

Section 615(b) of the Fair Credit Reporting Act applies whenever:
- consumer credit is denied for personal, family or household purposes, or
- the charge for such credit is increased wholly or partly because of information obtained from a person other than a consumer reporting agency bearing upon your
  - credit worthiness
  - credit standing
  - credit capacity
  - character
  - general reputation
  - personal characteristics or mode of living

The user of such information must, within sixty (60) days, after your **written request** for the reasons for such adverse action, disclose the nature of the information to you. The user must clearly and accurately disclose to you your right to make such written request at the time such adverse action is communicated to you.

Note that the creditor may make this notice either orally or in writing to you of your right to make a written request to learn the nature of the information on which the adverse action was based. See Form 615(b).

Your Right To Monetary Damages From A Consumer Reporting Agency For Noncompliance With The Fair Credit Reporting Act

Sections 616 and 617 respectively of the Fair Credit Reporting Act establish liability on any Consumer Reporting Agency or user of information which **willfully** or **negligently** fails to comply with any of the requirements under the Act.

Penalty For Willful Noncompliance Section 616

The penalty for willful noncompliance is:
    1 - Actual damages sustained by you, **plus**
    2 - Such amount of punitive damages as the court may allow, **plus**
    3 - Costs of the action together with reasonable attorney's fees.

The key word here is 'willful'. Refusing to correct your file, to investigate an item, to delete information or include your consumer statement would be examples of willful failure to comply with the Act.

Furthermore, a credit grantor or user of consumer reports who refuses to disclose to you the name and address of the Credit Reporting Agency issuing a consumer report resulting in a denial of credit to you would constitute "willful noncompliance".

Punitive damages are penalties assessed against the Credit Reporting Agency to punish its deficient behavior and to deter it from future violations.

The presence of punitive damages designed to punish the willful noncomplier makes penalties under Section 616 quite severe. See the Form Of Complaint.

Penalty For Negligent Noncompliance Section 617

The penalty for negligent noncompliance is:
1 - Actual damages sustained by you, **plus**
2 - Costs of the action together with reasonable attorney's fees.

Note that "negligent" noncompliance is a lesser degree of noncompliance than "willful" noncompliance. "Negligent" noncompliance is much harder for you to prove because the consumer reporting agency merely has to use reasonable procedures in compiling the information in your consumer report. In order to prove negligence, you would have to show deviance from that reasonable standard.

Also, costs and attorney's fees (after completion of a successful action) are to be determined by the court and may not be forthcoming on settlement of either a willful or negligent noncompliance case. See the Form Of Complaint.

A Defense Exists For Defamation Or Invasion Of Privacy Unless Willful Or Malicious Or Published With Malice

Except as provided in Sections 616 (willful noncompliance) and 617 (negligent noncompliance), you **can only** bring any action or proceeding in the nature of defamation and/or invasion of privacy against any Consumer Reporting Agency, any user of information or any person who furnishes information to a consumer reporting agency, **where there is false information furnished with malice or willful intent to injure you.**

Thus, you cannot sue a Consumer Reporting Agency or user for defamation or invasion of privacy as a result of information disclosed as required by the Fair Credit Reporting Act unless they willfully or maliciously report false information. This is a very difficult matter to prove. The litigious person is better advised to bring an action for willful or negligent compliance. See Form Of Complaint in this manual.

Jurisdiction Of Courts Section 618 of the Act

A consumer may sue under the Fair Credit Reporting Act in any United States District Court where you reside, or the Consumer Reporting Agency, or creditor-user resides, without regard to the amount in controversy.

NOTE: It is easier for you to sue in the district where you reside.

You may also sue in any other court of competent jurisdiction.

Section 618 puts a two (2) year statute of limitations beginning on the date when the liability arises.

The two year time limit in which to bring action is waived if the defendant **materially** and **willfully misrepresents** any information required to be disclosed to you. In that case, the two year time limit in which to bring action begins when the misrepresentation is discovered by you.

Since attorney's fees are receivable for violations of the Fair Credit Reporting Act, you should have little trouble in retaining counsel to bring an action for you. See the Form - Complaint To Bring Your Own Lawsuit.

If you wish, you may represent yourself. A form of complaint for violation of the Fair Credit Reporting Act is included in this manual. Consult the Court Clerk for fees and other procedures necessary for you to proceed pro se (for yourself, i.e. without counsel).

Negotiate with your creditors and credit reporting agencies before you sue without counsel.

CAUTION: The form of complaint in this manual is not a nuclear bomb to be dropped on creditors or Consumer Reporting Agencies. Negotiate and continue to negotiate to achieve your goals.

Consider litigation as a last resort just as war is the final resort of failed diplomacy.

Relation To State Laws

Section 622 of the Fair Credit Reporting Act provides for Federal supersession of the Act over inconsistent State laws. However, State laws which are not in violation of the Act are still in effect.

For example, under New York State law, a Consumer Reporting Agency must send any necessary correction of credit report information to all customer-users to whom inaccurate items of information were previously reported notwithstanding the six month time limit in the Fair Credit Reporting Act. This law is valid because it is not in conflict with the Federal law.

This manual deals primarily with the Fair Credit Collection Act. You should also verify what laws, if any, your state or city government has passed for your additional protection.

New York State, for example, has a New York Credit Reporting Act, N.Y. General Business Law, Section 380 through 385, which is patterned after the Federal law.

Part VI - The Importance Of A Major Credit Card

A major credit card is the key to obtaining valid credit references. Try to rent a car or check into a hotel without a major credit card and you will feel like a displaced person without a passport in the movie *Casablanca*.

Basically, the major credit card serves as the second proof of identification after or along with a driver's license. The credit card represents the golden key to the wonderful world of credit.

How To Obtain A Major Credit Card

The publisher of this manual has arranged with First National Bank of Marin (the "Bank") to issue a credit card to every purchaser of this manual who meets the virtually minimal requirements of maintaining a depository relationship with the Bank and otherwise conforms to the Bank's credit policies and procedures. In other words, anyone who opens up an account with the Bank can get a major credit card,(Subject to Bank approval.)

Form Bank-1 is a credit disclosure to you mandated by the Federal Reserve Board.

Form Bank-2 is the Bank's credit application for the card. Carefully read the entire application including the summary of credit terms so you will understand all the costs related to obtaining credit. The Bank will charge you the same fees as it does with all its other cardholders.

The Bank has agreed to give every qualified purchaser of this manual an initial line of credit equal to the deposit balance maintained in your account, if you meet their lending criteria.

The three 'C's of credit:
- Character - your credit history and the likelihood that you will be a person of such substantial integrity that the loan will be repaid.
- Capital - your assets.
- Capacity - your income from all established and continuing sources resulting in positive cash flow for debt service and loan repayment, after deducting your living expenses.

The three 'C's are often referred to by bankers as:
- Character,
- Character and
- Character !

because only people of substance and integrity will repay the loan when the going gets rough.

So fill out and return the Bank's Form-2 and hopefully, you will meet the Bank's credit procedures and policy and receive your major credit card.

Women, see For Women Only - Part VII to have your own credit history, and get a credit card in your own name.

Part VII - For Women Only: Obtaining Credit In Your Own Name

Very often a credit grantor records the credit file with the consumer reporting agency in the credit file name of the husband only, even though the loan and credit are jointly granted and are from joint assets.

The Consequences

After divorce or death of the husband, the wife discovers that she has no credit history.

Form Equal Opportunity Credit Act-1 addressed to each credit grantor, should serve to have the credit file reported to Consumer Reporting Agencies in **your** name **and** your husband's name.

How To Piggy Back On Your Joint Credit History To Get Your Own Credit Card History

At the wife's request, a Consumer Reporting Agency will arrange to have a file opened in the wife's own name. Her file will include:

1 - Her personal accounts
2 - Her husband's accounts which she uses
3 - Accounts in her husband's name where she is contractually liable for payment, or
4 - Accounts in her husband's name where "community property" guarantees payment.

It is crucial for the wife to contact each **credit grantor** directly to request that each credit grantor report the account history in both the wife's name and the husband's name.

Otherwise, the wife's new file is never updated because current information from subscriber creditors never comes to the credit bureaus in her name to be entered in her new file.

If she has her own income, it is strongly recommended that a woman apply for major credit cards in her own name.

Send Equal Opportunity Credit Act Form-1 To Each Creditor.

PART VIII - THE FORMS

Settlement Agreement Form Creditor 1 51
Request For A Copy Of Your Investigative Consumer Report - Form 606 53
Request For Deletion Of Obsolete Information - Form 607 54
Request For Personal Interview With Consumer Reporting Agency - Form 610 55
Request For Telephone Interview With
Consumer Reporting Agency - Form 610(b)(2) 56
Notice Of Disputed Claim To The Credit Reporting Agency - Form 611(a) 57
Form Of Consumer Statement - Form 611(b) 58
Your Request To The Consumer Reporting Agency To Furnish
Notification Of Deletion Of Disputed Items Or The Filing Of A
Consumer Statement To Any Person Who Received The Prior
Consumer Report (Made Within 30 Days After Notification Of
Adverse Credit Decision) - Form 611(d) 59
Your Request To The Consumer Reporting Agency To Furnish
Notification Of Deletion Of Disputed Items Or The Filing Of A
Consumer Statement To Any Person Who Received The Prior
Consumer Report (Made After 30 Days From Notification Of
Adverse Credit Decision) - Form 611(d)-2 60
Consumer's Written Request For Reasons For Adverse Action - Form 615(b) 61
Letter To The Federal Trade Commission - Letter 1 62
Letter To State Or County Consumer Protection Agency - Letter 2 63
Letter To Better Busines Bureau - Letter 3 64
Complaint And Demand For Jury Trial 65
First National Bank of Marin VISA/MasterCard Application (Form Bank–1 and Bank–2) .. 66
Equal Opportunity Act - Form-1 68
Request To Consumer Reporting Agency To Verify New Data
To Be Added To Your Credit File - Supplemental-1 69
Satisfaction Of Judgment 70
Discontinuance Of Action 72
Order Vacating Judgment 74
Taxpayer's Statement In Support Of An Offer In Compromise To IRS 76
Order To Show Cause 78
Affidavit In Support Of Order To Show Cause 80

SPECIFIC INSTRUCTIONS FOR FILLING IN NUMBERED BLANKS OF THE SETTLEMENT AGREEMENT FORM CREDITOR 1

Each of the numbers listed below corresponds to a number in parentheses on the sample form printed on the next page. The numbers on the sample form identify blank spaces that you will have to either fill-in with the appropriate information or dash out (--). The descriptions in this packet following the identifying numbers will tell you exactly what goes into each space on the blank form.

INSERT:

1 - Day

2 - Month

3 - Year
These comprise the date of the agreement.

4 - Your name

5 - Your address

6 - Creditor's name

7 - Creditor's address

8 - Entire settlement amount

9 - Monthly payment

10 - Day of the month by which you will pay

11 - Day

12 - Month

13 - Year
Day first payment is due

14 - Your signature

15 - Creditor's signature

FORM CREDITOR 1
SETTLEMENT AGREEMENT

AGREEMENT made this ____(1)__ day of _____(2)_____, 19 _(3)_ between _____(4)_____ (debtor) residing at _____(5)_____, and _____(6)_____ (creditor), having an office at _____(7)_____.
(creditor's address including street, state and zip code).

WHEREAS, Debtor and Creditor have previously entered into a certain commercial transaction, and

WHEREAS, certain circumstances had subsequently developed causing both Debtor and Creditor to desire to enter into this agreement.

NOW THEREFORE based upon the mutual promises contained herein.

IT IS AGREED:

1 - Debtor agrees to pay and creditor agrees to accept $__(8)_____ as full payment for all amounts owed by Debtor to Creditor.

2 - Debtor shall be permitted to pay the aforesaid sum by monthly payments without interest at the rate of $ ___(9)_____ per month. All of the monthly payments are to be made by mail or otherwise at the office of the Creditor set forth above prior to the __(10)_ day of each month commencing the _(11)_ day of __(12)___, 19 (13)_

3 - In the event of a default by Debtor in making any of the above stated payments, the Creditor shall have the right upon ten (10) days written notice to Debtor, to declare the unpaid installments due hereunder immediately due and payable.

4 - Creditor agrees to notify each credit bureau with whom creditor deals that adverse information regarding Debtor's account is no longer verifiable and should be deleted from Debtor's consumer report.

IN WITNESS WHEREOF, the Debtor and Creditor have signed this agreement as of the date set forth above.

_____(14)_____
(Debtor)

_____(15)_____
(Creditor)

FORM 606

REQUEST FOR A COPY OF YOUR
INVESTIGATIVE CONSUMER REPORT

Date

Consumer Reporting Agency Name
Street Address
City, State, Zip Code

RE: Request for a copy of my Investigative Consumer Report

Gentlemen:

Reference is made to an Investigative Consumer Report concerning me recently requested by your organization.

Please be advised that a request is hereby made by me for a complete and accurate disclosure of the nature and source of the investigation on me.

Please be further advised that this request is made pursuant to Section 606 of the Federal Fair Credit Reporting Act which mandates a response by you within five (5) days.

Very truly yours,

_____

Your signature, name, and address

FORM 607

REQUEST FOR DELETION OF OBSOLETE INFORMATION

Date

Credit Reporting Agency
Street Address
City, State, Zip Code

Re: Request for Deletion of Obsolete Information

Gentlemen:

Reference is made to your obligation under Sections 605 and 607 of the Federal Fair Credit Reporting Act to delete obsolete information from the consumer credit report of the undersigned.

Please be advised that the information circled on the attached copy of the consumer credit report is obsolete and should be deleted from your credit files relating to the undersigned.

Please delete this information immediately.

Very truly yours,

_____
Your name

_____
Your address

FORM 610 - REQUEST FOR PERSONAL INTERVIEW WITH CONSUMER REPORTING AGENCY

Date

Consumer Reporting Agency
Street Address
City, State, Zip Code

RE: Request for Personal Interview

Gentlemen:

Pursuant to Sections 609 and 610 of the Federal Fair Credit Reporting Act, the undersigned request(s) the favor of a personal interview with your organization for the purpose of obtaining a copy of the consumer credit report issued by you and reviewing your files for a clear and accurate disclosure of the nature and scope of all information concerning the undersigned.

The undersigned proposes to appear at your office on _(Fill-in day, month, and year)_ at _(Fill-in time)_ A.M./P.M. If this date or time is not acceptable to you, please advise so that a mutually agreeable date and/or time may be arranged.

Within the last thirty (30) days, the undersigned has *(has not) received:

(a) A debt collection notice from an affiliate of your organization, or

(b) Notice of an adverse credit determination either denying credit or increasing charges wholly or partly as a result of a credit report from your organization.

Accordingly, a fee is (is not) due to your organization. If you claim that a fee is due, please advise as to the amount.

Please have the files of the undersigned ready for review.

Very truly yours,

* Fees may be payable after 30 days
  from receipt of such notice

_____

Your name
Your address

FORM 610 (b)(2)
REQUEST FOR TELEPHONE INTERVIEW WITH CONSUMER REPORTING AGENCY
Date

Credit Reporting Agency
Street Address
City, State, Zip Code

RE: Written Request for Telephone Interview

Gentlemen:

    Pursuant to Section 610(b)(2) of the Federal Fair Credit Reporting Act, the undersigned hereby requests(s) the favor of a telephone interview with your organization for the purpose of obtaining a copy of the consumer report issued by you and reviewing your files for a clear and accurate disclosure of the nature and scope of all information concerning the undersigned.
    As proper identification, the following is tendered:

(Fill-in the   1 - Name _____
identifying   2 - Spouse's Name _____
information)   3 - Current Address _____
                4 - Previous Address (if at current address less than five (5) years)_____
                _____
                5 - Date of Birth _____
                6 - Social Security Number _____

Please furnish the undersigned with the telephone number of your agency's interview department so that the undersigned can call and request answers or furnish supplemental information to augment your file.
    Within the last thirty (30) days, the undersigned has *(has not) received:
    (a) A debt collection notice from an affiliate of your organization, or
    (b) Notice of an adverse credit determination denying credit or increasing charges wholly or partly as a result of a credit report from your organization.
    Accordingly, a fee is (is not) due to your organization. If you claim that a fee is due, please advise as to the amount.
    You may reach the undersigned at __(Fill-in your phone number)__ during normal business hours and you may (may not) call collect.

                                            Very truly yours,

                                            _____

                                            Your name

                                            _____

                                            Your address

*Fee may be payable after 30 days
 from receipt of such notice.

FORM 611(a)

NOTICE OF DISPUTED CLAIM TO
THE CREDIT REPORTING AGENCY

Date

Credit Reporting Agency
Street Address
City, State, Zip Code

RE: Notice of Disputed Accuracy Pursuant to
Section 611 of the Federal Fair Credit
Reporting Act

Gentlemen:

PLEASE TAKE NOTICE, that the undersigned hereby disputes the completeness and accuracy of the following information currently maintained in your files concerning the undersigned:

(Fill-in   NAME OF CREDITOR_____
information)   ITEM OF INFORMATION_____
                AMOUNT ALLEGEDLY OWED_____

The particulars of the dispute are as follows:

1 - The undersigned does not owe the account and disputes the charges.

2 - Other: ___(Fill-in particulars)_____
_____

Please reinvestigate and if the disputed information is found to be inaccurate, or can no longer be verified, promptly delete the information from the consumer report of the undersigned.

Very truly yours,

_____
Your signature
Your name and
address

FORM 611(b)

FORM OF CONSUMER STATEMENT

Date

Credit Reporting Agency
Street Address
City, State, Zip Code

RE: Consumer Statement

Gentlemen:

Reference is made to the following information currently maintained in your files concerning the undersigned:

NAME OF CREDITOR_____
ITEM OF INFORMATION_____
AMOUNT ALLEGEDLY OWED_____

PLEASE BE ADVISED, that the undersigned vigorously disputes the truth of such information and interposes the following consumer statement:

THE UNDERSIGNED DOES NOT OWE THE ACCOUNT AND DISPUTES THE CHARGE.

OTHER: (FILL-IN PARTICULARS)_____

PLEASE BE FURTHER ADVISED, that pursuant to Section 611(b) of the Federal Fair Credit Reporting Act, the undersigned requests that you update your records to provide a copy of such CONSUMER STATEMENT or a clear and accurate codification or summary thereof.

Very truly yours,

_____
Your name and address

FORM 611(d)

YOUR REQUEST TO THE CONSUMER REPORTING AGENCY TO FURNISH NOTIFICATION OF DELETION OF DISPUTED ITEMS OR THE FILING OF A CONSUMER STATEMENT TO ANY PERSON WHO RECEIVED THE PRIOR CONSUMER REPORT - MADE WITHIN 30 DAYS AFTER NOTIFICATION OF ADVERSE CREDIT DECISION

Date

Credit Reporting Agency
Street Address
City, State, Zip Code

Re: Notification

Gentlemen:

Pursuant to Section 611(d) of the Federal Fair Credit Reporting Act, the undersigned hereby requests that you notify every person who has personally received the deleted or disputed information within the past two (2) years, that such information has been subsequently deleted, or that a consumer statement disputing the claim has been appended to the file.

This request is made within thirty (30) days after receipt by the undersigned of (a) an adverse credit determination, or (b) notification from a debt collection agency affiliated with your organization.

Accordingly, <u>no fee</u> is due.

Very truly yours,

_____
Your name and address

FORM 611 (d)-2

YOUR REQUEST TO THE CONSUMER REPORTING AGENCY TO FURNISH NOTIFICATION OF DELETION OF DISPUTED ITEMS OR THE FILING OF A CONSUMER STATEMENT TO ANY PERSON WHO RECEIVED THE PRIOR CONSUMER REPORT - MADE AFTER 30 DAYS FROM NOTIFICATION OF ADVERSE CREDIT DECISION

Date

Consumer Reporting Agency
Street Address
City, State, Zip Code

Re: Notification

Gentlemen:

Pursuant to Section 611(d) of the Federal Fair Credit Reporting Act, the undersigned hereby requests that you notify any person who previously received the deleted or disputed information within the past two (2) years that such information has been subsequently deleted or that a consumer statement disputing the claim has been appended to the file.

This request is not made within thirty (30) days after receipt by the undersigned of (a) an adverse credit determination, or (b) notification from a debt collection agency affiliated with your organization.

Accordingly, if a fee is due you, please advise the amount of such fee for said notification.

Very truly yours,

_____

Your name and address

FORM 615(b)

CONSUMER'S WRITTEN REQUEST FOR REASONS FOR ADVERSE ACTION

Date

User of Credit Information
Street Address
City, State, Zip Code

RE: Consumer's Written Request for the Reasons for Adverse Action

Gentlemen:

Reference is made to your adverse credit decision concerning the undersigned.

PLEASE TAKE NOTICE, that pursuant to Section 615(b) of the Federal Fair Credit Reporting Act, the undersigned hereby requests a clear and accurate disclosure of the factual information disclosed to you by persons other than Consumer Reporting Agencies concerning the undersigned. Such information should be in sufficient detail so as to allow the undersigned to refute, challenge or dispute its accuracy.

PLEASE TAKE FURTHER NOTICE, that you are required to render such notification to the undersigned within a reasonable time.

Very truly yours,

_____
Your name and address

LETTER 1

LETTER TO THE FEDERAL TRADE COMMISSION

Date

Federal Trade Commission
Fair Credit Reporting Act
Washington, D.C. 20580

Gentlemen:

The undersigned understands that you regulate Consumer Reporting Agencies pursuant to the Fair Credit Reporting Act (The Act), and wishes to lodge a complaint against the following agency:

NAME OF CREDIT BUREAU_____
ADDRESS OF CREDIT BUREAU_____

This credit bureau has refused to comply with its obligations under The Act. The substance of the complaint is as follows:

(insert complaint, i.e. Agency won't amend my credit report, or agency doesn't respond to my letters., etc.)

Your organization is hereby notified so that you may be aware of and able to act upon a matter of abuse of that Consumer Reporting Act.

The undersigned would be happy to furnish full particulars to you if you need further information for enforcement proceedings.

Very truly yours,

_____
Your name and address

LETTER 2

LETTER TO STATE OR COUNTY CONSUMER PROTECTION AGENCY

Date

Name of State or County Agency
Street Address
City, State, Zip Code

Gentlemen:

The undersigned hereby lodges a consumer complaint against the following credit bureau:

NAME OF AGENCY_____
ADDRESS OF CREDIT AGENCY_____

This credit bureau has refused to comply with its obligations under the Federal Fair Credit Reporting Act. The substance of the complaint is as follows:

(Insert complaint, i.e. Agency won't amend my credit report, or agency won't return to my phone calls., etc.)

Your organization is hereby notified of such complaint so that (a) you may be aware of a pattern of abuse, and (b) you may take enforcement proceedings.

The undersigned would be happy to furnish full particulars to you if you need further information for enforcement proceedings.

Very truly yours,

_____
Your name and address

LETTER 3

LETTER TO BETTER BUSINESS BUREAU

Date

Better Business Bureau
Street Address
City, State, Zip Code

Gentlemen:

The undersigned hereby lodges a complaint against the following bureau:

NAME OF AGENCY:_____
ADDRESS OF AGENCY:_____

This credit bureau has refused to comply with its obligations under the Federal Fair Credit Reporting Act. The substance of the complaint is as follows:

(Insert the complaint, i.e. Agency won't amend my credit report, or agency won't respond to correspondence., etc.,)

Your organization is hereby notified of such complaint so that (a) you may be aware of a pattern of abuse, and (b) you may take action to help consumers.

The undersigned would be happy to furnish full particulars to you if you need additional information.

Very truly yours,

_____
Your name and address

UNITED STATES DISTRICT COURT
DISTRICT OF

YOUR NAME	:	
Plaintiff	:	Civil Action No. (to be obtained from Court)
	:	
against	:	COMPLAINT and
	:	DEMAND FOR JURY
	:	TRIAL
INSERT NAME OF	:	
CREDIT REPORTING AGENCY	:	
	:	
Defendant.	:	

I. INTRODUCTION

1. This is an action for statutory damages brought by an individual consumer for Defendant's violations of the Fair Credit Reporting Act, 15 U.S.C. Section 1601 et seq., (hereinafter 'FCRA'), which prohibits consumer reporting agencies from engaging in willful or negligent credit reporting practices.

II. JURISDICTION

2. Jurisdiction of this Court arises under 15 U.S.C. Sections 1681e, 1681n and 1681o.

III. PARTIES

3. Plaintiff, (your name)_____, is a natural person residing in (your city and state).

4. Defendant, (name of credit bureau), is a consumer reporting agency with a principal place of business located at (address of credit bureau). The Defendant is a credit reporting agency.

IV. FACTUAL ALLEGATIONS

5. On or about (date), Defendant willfully and or negligently failed to comply with requirements imposed upon it under the FCRA in that Defendant refused to update, amend or supplement and otherwise correct its credit files relating to Plaintiff and inform Plaintiff's creditors of Plaintiff's proposed changes to such files.

V. FIRST CLAIM FOR RELIEF

6. Plaintiff repeats and realleges and incorporates by reference paragraphs one through five above.
7. Defendant violated the FCRA. Defendant's violations include, but are not limited to, the following:
   (a) The Defendant violated 15 U.S.C. Section 1681n willfully by failing to include Plaintiff's corrections in its credit files and failing to notify Plaintiff's creditors of such changes as required by The Act.
   (b) The Defendant violated 15 U.S.C. Section 1681o by negligently failing to include Plaintiff's correction in its credit files and failing to notify Plaintiff's creditors of such changes as required by The Act.
   (c) The Defendant violated 15 U.S.C. Section 1681e by failing to maintain reasonable compliance procedures designed to avoid violations of the FCRA.
8. As a result of the above violations of the FCRA, the Defendant is liable to the Plaintiff for statutory and punitive damages, as well as costs and attorney's fees.

WHEREFORE, Plaintiff respectfully prays that Judgment be entered against the Defendant in the amount of:
   (a) _____ Thousand Dollars ($_____) statutory damages pursuant to 15 U.S.C. Section 1681n and 1681o.
   (b) Punitive damages in the amount of $_____ pursuant to 15 U.S.C. Section 1681n.
   (c) Costs and reasonable attorney's fees pursuant to 15 U.S.C. Section 1681n and Section 1681o.
   (d) For such other and further relief as may be just and proper.

DATED:

Respectfully submitted,

_____
Your name

_____
Your address

PRO SE

THE VISA/MASTERCARD ALMOST ANYONE CAN QUALIFY FOR

Would you like the convenience and prestige of having your own VISA or MasterCard, regardless of your credit experience? Now ther's an easy way for you to get your own VISA/MasterCard - even if you've had trouble qualifying before!

ESTABLISH OR RE-ESTABLISH YOUR CREDIT

Even if you have no credit history, have low income, or have had credit problems in the past (even bankruptcy!), federally insured First National Bank of Marin can help you establish a new credit history with a Secured VISA or MasterCard.

SECURED CREDIT - THE EASY SOLUTION

The First National Bank Secured Credit Card is issued in a combination savings and credit program. And the good news is almost everyone is approved who can answer "YES" to these simple questions:
- Are you 18 years or older?
- Do you have a combined household income of $1,000 per month or more?
- Will you open a minimum $300 savings account with First National Bank of Marin?

A PARTNER TO HELP YOU WHEN OTHERS CAN'T

If your answers are "YES" - CONGRATULATIONS! The First National Bank of Marin is ready to work as your partner in credit. Our quick, convenient and confidential bank-by-mail process will allow you to begin building a nest egg for your family and a solid credit history - benefits that will last a lifetime! Take your choice of VISA or MasterCard - or both - and begin enjoying the freedom and convenience that having your own credit card can bring.

THE PRIVILEGES AND BENEFITS YOU DESERVE

As a First National Bank of Marin cardholder, you'll join the ranks of thousands of people special enough to carry VISA/MasterCard. With your own credit card you can soon be enjoying all the benefits of card-membership including:
- Worldwide shopping convenience at more than 6 million locations
- Instant cash at more than 350,000 financial institutions and automated teller machines
- Identification for cashing checks or making travel arrangements

IT'S EASY TO APPLY

Complete the application, enclose your check or money order for the required application fee, and mail it to the Service Center. Upon receipt, we will send you your savings account signature card to sign and return along with your opening deposit. Once your savings account is established and you have met the other requirements we will send you your own VISA/MasterCard.

SET YOUR OWN CREDIT LIMIT

You can open your savings account with as little as $300 or any amount up to $5,000 - it's your choice. Your credit card will be issued with a credit limit equal "dollar for dollar" to the amount you have on deposit. You may add to your savings account anytime and we'll increase your credit limit. Watch your savings grow while you establish good credit!

MONEY BACK APPROVAL GUARANTEE
If for any reason you don't qualify, we'll refund your application fee in full! APPLYING IS RISK FREE!

APPLYING IS AS EASY AS 1-2-3!

1. **Complete and Sign the Application.** Please use a pen and print clearly. Read the entire form before signing. Joint applications must also be signed by co-applicant. **BE SURE TO ENTER TOTAL FEE ENCLOSED.**
2. **Insert Check or Money Order.** We won't be able to accept your application unless you enclose payment in full for the correct fees in an envelope, payable to "The BankCard Service Center". Enclosing required proof of income will speed processing.
3. **Seal and Mail.** Seal the envelope and mail to:

THE BANKCARD SERVICE CENTER
Post Office Box 3696
San Clemente, CA 92674
1-800-727-3622

APPLICATION

- ☐ VISA ☐ MASTERCARD
- ☐ ONE CARD $60 ☐ BOTH CARDS $80
- ☐ CO-APPLICANT CARD $10 EACH

TOTAL ENCLOSED $

PLEASE TELL US ABOUT YOURSELF
Note: You must be 18 years of age to apply

Name / Date of Birth

Address

City / State / Zip

Phone / Soc. Sec.#

☐ Own home
☐ Rent
Mo. Yr. / How Long?

PLEASE TELL US ABOUT YOUR WORK
NOTE: Pay stub or other proof of income required

Employer / Phone

Employer Address

Position / How Long?

Mo. Salary / Other / Source

PLEASE TELL US ABOUT A CO-APPLICANT (Optional)

Name / Relation

Address / Phone

City / State / Zip

Employer / Mo. Salary / Soc. Sec.#

SIGNATURE / DATE

CO-APPLICANT / DATE

IMPORTANT INFORMATION! PLEASE READ CAREFULLY

The following information and agreement contain the conditions under which you apply for credit through The BankCard Service Center. The work "card" will mean VISA, MasterCard or both if you have applied for multiple cards. The word "I" and "my" will mean the applicant applying for credit, and will also include the co-applicant when appropriate. "BankCard Center" will mean The BankCard Service Center. "FNBM" will mean First National Bank of Marin of San Rafael, California, the card issuing institution, or other card issuer offering a similar program as selected by BankCard Center.

By signing this Application and by paying the application fee you agree to the following:

AGREEMENT

I certify under penalty of perjury that the information contained in this application is true and correct. I have enclosed the one-time application fee indicated, based on the number and type of card(s) I have requested. I understand that BankCard Center reserves the right to decline this application at any time, and that if I a denied approval my application fee will be refunded in full with the denial letter.

I agree to open and maintain a savings account at FNBM with a minimum balance of at least three hundred dollars ($300) up to a maximum of $5,000.00 to secure my credit card account. My savings account balance will earn interest at the current rate for credit card savings accounts in effect from time-to-time a FNBM. My savings account balance must be at least equal to my credit limit for my credit card at all times. If I meet the initial requirements for approval, but fail to make the required savings deposit, my application fee will be forfeited and no card will be issued.

I authorize BankCard Center to obtain a credit report and to verify and exchang credit information about me with third parties, including credit bureaus. I agree to provide additional information as requested by FNBM or BankCard Center from time-to-time. I understand you will retain this application and any credit or other information you receive, whether or not my application is approved.

If I am issued a card, my acceptance of it will indicate my agreement to pay all charges incurred in accordance with the terms of the Cardholder Agreement that will be sent to me with the card, and any future amendments to the Agreement. A summary of certain credit terms is provided below.

SUMMARY OF CREDIT TERMS

Here is a summary of certain credit terms that will govern use of your credit card account. These terms are subject to change from time-to-time, at FNBM's sole discretion, upon notice to you as required by law.

Credit terms are valid as of the date of printing. Write or call BankCard Center at the number on the application for updated terms.

Annual Percentage Rate	Balance Calculation Method for Purchases	Membership Fees	Late Payment & Over Limit Fees **
19.8%	Average Daily Balance including new transactions	Annual: $25 Application * $60-100	Late Fee $15 Over Limit Fee $15
Grace period for Purchases	**Minimum Funance Charge**	**Transaction Fee for Purchases**	**Transaction Fee for Cash Advances**
25 days from statement date	$.50	None	$2.00 or 3% of advance, whichever is greater

* The Application Fee is a "FINANCE CHARGE" for truth in lending purposes.
** Returned checks are subject to a $15 fee.

NOTICE OF CANCELLATION

You may cancel this application at any time prior to midnight of the fifth day after the date of the transaction. If you cancel, your fee will be returned with 30 days following receipt. Cancellation must be in writing to the address immediately above the application.

Credit cards are issued by First National Bank of Marin (FNBM)
1120 Nye Street, San Rafael, California 94901
The BankCard Service Center is the Credit Card Service Center for FNBM
Secured Credit Plan is a registered trademark of ASCS, Inc.
VISA is a registered trademark of VISA International Service Association
MasterCard is a registered trademark of MasterCard International, Inc.

EQUAL OPPORTUNITY ACT FORM-1

Date

Creditor's Name
Creditor's Street Address
City, State, Zip Code

Gentlemen:

Reference is made to those provisions of the Equal Opportunity Credit Act which allow credit information to be maintained in separate files of each of a husband and wife.

Please be advised that the undersigned hereby requests that credit information on the accounts of the undersigned be maintained by you in separate files under each name.

Please be further advised that we request this information be made available to all credit reporting agencies.

Very truly yours,

Account #_____

_____
Husband

_____
Wife

_____
Address

**REMEMBER, SEND ONE (1) COPY OF THIS FORM
TO EVERY CREDITOR.**

SUPPLEMENTAL-1

REQUEST TO CONSUMER REPORTING AGENCY TO VERIFY NEW DATA TO BE ADDED TO YOUR CREDIT FILE

Date

Credit Reporting Agency
Street Address
City, State, Zip Code

Re: Request to Add Data to Consumer Report

Gentlemen:

Pursuant to the Fair Credit Reporting Act, you are hereby requested to add the following data to the consumer credit report of the undersigned:

(Insert data, i.e.
 gasoline credit card
 credit union account)

Please advise as to the amount, if any, of your fee for verifying and including this data on all new consumer reports issued by you.

Very truly yours,

_____
Your name and address

Social Security Number_____
Date Of Birth_____

Instructions To Complete Satisfaction Of Judgment

1 - Insert Index number

2 - Insert Name of Court as it appears in Summons and Complaint including County and State

3 - Insert Name of Creditor

4 - Insert Your Name

5 - Insert State

6 - Insert County

7 - Insert Amount Paid

8 - Insert date Judgment was originally entered

9 - Insert Name of Plaintiff

10 - Insert Name of Signatory

11 - Insert Name and Address of Attorney for Plaintiff

12 - Insert State

13 - Insert County

14 - Insert Name of Signatory for Plaintiff

15 - Insert Address of Plaintiff's Signatory

16 - Insert Name of Notary Public

Court of The ①
County of ②

③
Plaintiff

against

④
Defendant(s)

Satisfaction of Judgment

State of ⑤
County of ⑥ } ss.:

Satisfaction is hereby acknowledged between plaintiff, and the above named defendant, for the sum of

Judgment entered in the Judgment Book of the above Court on ⑧

Attest:

⑨
By
⑩

Assistant Secretary

⑪
Attorney for Plaintiff

State of ⑫
County of ⑬ } ss.:

On ⑭ before me personally came to me known, who being duly sworn did depose and say that he resides in

That he is the ⑮ of the corporation described in and which executed the above instrument; that he knew the seal affixed to said instrument was such corporate seal; that it was so affixed by order of the Board of Directors of said corporation, and that he signed his name thereto by like order.

⑯

Form 1

Instructions For Discontinuance Of Action

1 - Insert Index Number

2 - Insert County of Court

3 - Insert State

4 - Insert Name of Plaintiff

5 - Insert Your Name

6 - Insert Rate

7 - Insert Name and Address of Plaintiff's Attorney

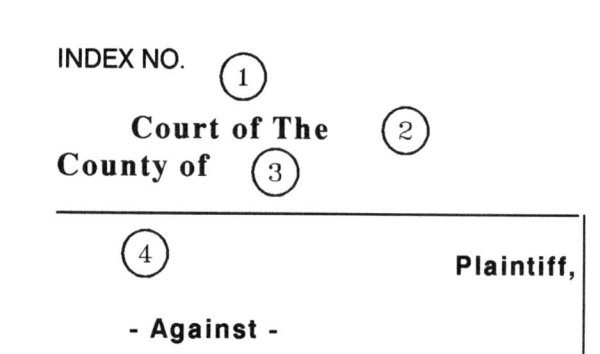

INDEX NO. ① ②

Court of The ③
County of

④

Plaintiff,

- Against -

⑤

Defendant(s)

The within action is hereby discontinued.

Dated:
⑥

⑦

Attorney for Plaintiff

Discontinuance of Action

INSTRUCTIONS FOR COMPLETING ORDER VACATING JUDGMENT

1 - Insert Index Number

2 - Insert County where Court is located

3 - Insert State where Court is located

4 - Insert Name of Plaintiff

5 - Insert Your Name

6 - Insert Name of Attorney for Plaintiff

7 - Insert Date Judgment was entered

8 - Insert Amount of Judgment

9 - Insert Name of Plaintiff's Attorney

10 - Insert Address of Courthouse

11 - Insert Date

12 - Insert Name of Plaintiff

13 - Insert Your Name

14 - Insert Name of Plaintiff's Attorney

15 - Insert Date

16 - Insert Name of Plaintiff's Attorney

The FORM on the opposite page is a type of statement used in support of the facts relevant to an Offer In Compromise.

The facts in your statement, of course will be different because your statement will reflect your own individual circumstances.

INDEX NO. ①
② COURT OF
COUNTY OF ③

```
┌─────────────────────────────────────┐
│            ④          Plaintiff,    │
│         - against -                 │
│            ⑤                        │
│                       Defendant.    │
└─────────────────────────────────────┘
```

ORDER VACATING JUDGMENT

STATE OF   )
) ss.:
COUNTY OF   )

⑥ affirms under penalty of perjury and says:

That I am an attorney admitted to practice in New York State and the attorney for the plaintiff in the above-entitled action, and that Judgment was entered ⑦ in the above-named Court in the amount of $ ⑧ .

That defendant did not appear or answer either generally or specially but because of circumstances which have subsequently developed, it is the desire of the plaintiff to have the said Judgment vacated and set aside. No execution is outstanding.

WHEREFORE, your deponent on behalf of plaintiff requests that this Order be signed to vacate and set aside the above-mentioned Judgment for which no previous application has been made.

Affirmed: ⑨
_____

At a Special Term, Part II of the Civil Court of the City of New York,
at the Courthouse,
No.   ⑩
Dated ⑪

PRESENT:
   Hon.:   Judge.

```
┌─────────────────────────────────────┐
│            ⑫          Plaintiff,    │
│         - against -                 │
│            ⑬                        │
│                       Defendant.    │
└─────────────────────────────────────┘
```

Upon the affirmation of ⑭ dated ⑮ IT IS ON MOTION OF ⑯ , attorney for the plaintiff, ORDERED that the above Judgment be vacated and set aside and a copy of this Order be served on the defendant by certified mail within 15 days.

Enter: Judge of the Civil Court

Taxpayer's Statement In Support Of An Offer In Compromise To IRS

The Form on the opposite page is a type of statement used in support of the facts relevant to an Offer In Compromise.

The facts in your statement, of course will be different because your statement will reflect your own individual circumstances.

See the IRS Form 656 Offer In Compromise and the supporting IRS Form 433 Statement Of Financial Condition And Other Information which are the last two forms in this book.

Please attach your Taxpayer's Statement In Support Of An Offer In Compromise to IRS Forms 656 and Form 433 as part of your submission to the IRS.

TAXPAYER'S STATEMENT IN SUPPORT OF AN
OFFER IN COMPROMISE TO IRS

Taxpayer suffers from an mental disorder which her psychiatrist in the attached letter characterizes as a bi-polar disorder resulting in rapid cycling of episodes of depression and mania. As a result of this disorder, she is disabled and cannot hold a regular job. She was last hospitalized in November, 1986.

Taxpayer is unemployed and even though she tries, cannot hold a steady job. Accordingly, she is forced to live on a fixed income of her alimony.

As shown in the attached schedules, Taxpayer's reasonable and necessary living expenses equal, approach and can exceed her fixed income.

IRS collection efforts serve to heighten Taxpayer's anxiety, deepen her depression and worsen her mental condition. An unrelated female friend of Taxpayer, who is a widow, is willing to give Taxpayer, as a gift, the sum of $ 3,000.00 (to help cure Taxpayer's mental disorder), if the IRS will accept the $ 3,000.00 as an offer in compromise. The remainder of the offer in compromise is the deeding of the Taxpayer's only asset, i.e. the single shareof ABC Corp. to the IRS.

Therefore, the offer in compromise constitutes the Taxpayer giving to the IRS, all of her assets plus $ 3,000.00 in cash from an unrelated third party.

Taxpayer is also an alien, not a citizen of the United States, but a subject of Great Britain. There is a possibility that Taxpayer could return to England leaving the IRS with no ability to collect anything on this tax liability should the offer in compromise not be accepted.

Taxpayer requests a meeting with the IRS and her representative to further discuss this offer should same be helpful in resolving this matter.

Instructions To Order To Show Cause

FILL IN THE FOLLOWING INFORMATION

1. The index number of the case against you.

2. The year in the index number indicating the year the case was started.

3. The caption of the court, i.e. the name of the court

4. The county where the Court sits.

5. The name of the person who sued you.

6. Your name.

7. Your name or the name of the person making the accompanying affidavit.

8. The day, month and year on which the affidavit was sworn to before a notary public.

9. Enter his or her depending on the gender of the person who sued you.

10. The Part of the Court hearing the Order to Show Cause or the Room number where the case will be heard.

11. The address of the Courthouse.

12. The County in which the court sits.

13. The date, month and year the on which the court will hear the case.

14. The date, month and year the judgment was entered against you.

15. The date, month and year on or before which you must serve a copy of this order on the plaintiff.

16. The date the judge signs the order.

Note: MOST OF THE BODY OF THIS FORM WILL BE FILLED IN BY RUBBER STAMP BY COURT CLERK.

Index No._____ ② Year 19___
①

③ COURT OF
COUNTY OF ④

⑤

Plaintiff

against

⑥

Defendant

ORDER TO SHOW CAUSE

Upon the annexed affidavit of _____⑦_____ sworn to the ⑧ day of ___⑧___, 19___, the defendant above named, and on all the proceedings had herin, LET the plaintiff or h⑨ attorney show cause before me or one of the Judges of this Court, at Part ⑩ therof, to be held at the Courthouse thereof, located at ___⑪___, in the County of ___⑫___, City and State of ___⑫___ on the ⑬ day of ___⑬___, 19___, at _____ o'clock in the _____noon of that day, or as soon thereafter as counsel can be heard, WHY an order should not be made, vacating and setting aside the judgment entere herein, in favor of the plaintiff and against the defendant, on the ⑭ day of ___⑭___, 19___, and restoring the case to the calendar for trial on a day certain and why such other and further relie should not be granted as may be just in the premises.

Pending the hearing and determination of this motion and the entry of an order thereon, LET all proceedings on the part of the plaintiff, h___ attorneys and agents and any Marshal or Sheriff of the City of _____, for the enforcement of said judgment be stayed.

SUFFICIENT CAUSE THEREFOR APPEARING, LET service of a copy of this order, together with the affidavit annexed hereto on the plaintiff or h⑨ attorneys, on or before the ⑮ day of ___⑮___ 19___, be sufficient.

Dated, ___⑯___, 19___.

_____
Judge

Instructions To Affidavit In Support Of Order To Show Cause

Fill in the following information in the numbered blanks.

1. The caption of the court, i.e. the name of the court.
2. The county in which the court sits.
3. The index number and year of the case.
4. The name of the person who sued you.
5. Your name.
6. Your name.
7. Fill in the facts showing why you never knew the case was started against you.
8. State your defense
9. Your signature.
10. Your street address.
11. Your city, state, and zip code.

① COURT OF
COUNTY OF ②

④ Plaintiff

- against -

⑤ Defendant

Index No. ③ / 19 ③

_____⑥_____, being duly sworn, deposes and says:

⑦ I never received notice of this case.
I was never served with the summons and complaint.

I believe I have a meritorious defense in that

    I do not owe the money. ⑧

I respectfully request that the attached order be signed.

There has been no previous application for this relief except

_____⑨_____
Signature

_____⑩_____
Address

_____⑪_____
City, State & Zip Code